The Universe
Speaks

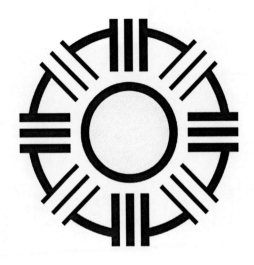

The Palmunwon

The Palmunwon is a representation of the Universe.
It is a tool which can be used to purify yourself and your surroundings. By meditating on and visualizing the Palmunwon,
you can help the Earth and your body and mind to prepare
for the Earth's ascension into the 5th dimension. You can also
expand your consciousness to include the whole universe.
Please meditate and pray on it daily and feel the energy of the
universe!

Palmunwon Prayer

I send my love to the Earth and all plants, animals, water and
soil and pray for their comfort and safety.
I pray for the evolution of the Earth, my neighbours and myself.
I send my gratitude to all creations.
I am thankful for this precious gift from the Universe.

The Universe Speaks

Speaks

"The Love and Pain of 2012 to 2025"

Roar Sheppard

Marlin

Published by

Kima Global Publishers

Kima Global House,

50, Clovelly Road,

Clovelly

7975

South Africa

© Roar Sheppard 2011

ISBN: 978-1-920533-05-2

First Edition

Email: info@kimaglobal.co.za

Web site: http://www.kimaglobal.co.za

This book has been compiled from the messages that Suseonjae
meditation practitioners have had with cosmic beings.
Roar Sheppard is the representative author. Conversation
with Gaia was written by Yeonmi Hong.

Table of Contents

Prologue	ix
Part One	1
Chapter 1: A Conversation with Mother Gaia	2
– Tears of Gaia	2
– The Relationship between Gaia and our Collective Unconscious	9
– Gaia's Message to Everyone on the Earth	11
Chapter 2: A Conversation with the Collective Unconscious of Humanity	15
– Human Consciousness has lost its Rudder	22
Chapter 3: The Earth that Cosmic Beings Speak of	29
– The Earth a very special Planet	29
– The Purpose of Earth's Creation	32
– The Earth's People are Foreign Students from other Planets	38
– Dimensional Ascension; the Planned Schedule for the Earth	41
– The Role of the Earth's people after the Ascension	46
Part Two	49
Chapter 4: The Earth's Dimensional Ascension and the Photon Belt	50
– The Earth of the 5th Dimension; will it be Possible?	50
– The Gate to the New Dimension; the Photon Belt	53

- Entering the Photon Belt and Dimensional
  Ascension   54
- A Magnetic Field is a Celestial Body's
  Photon Belt   57

Chapter 5: The Changes caused by the Entrance into the
Photon Belt   67

Part Three   73

Chapter 6: The Changes the Earth will face while
passing the Photon Belt   74
- Unusual Changes of Weather and Social
  Confusion   75

Chapter 7: The Conditions Before and After Entry
into the Photon Belt   90
- The Earth is a Creature that is Alive and
  Breathes   98

Chapter 8: The Forecast for the Crisis of Each
Continent   102
- The Crisis of Oceana   102
- The Crisis of Asia   102
- China in an Extremely Precarious
  State   107
- Japan: Extreme Natural Disasters in
  2011/2012   109
- Korea   111
- The Crisis of the Americas: North America 112
- The Crisis of Central and
  South America   117
- The Crisis of Africa   119
- The Crisis of Europe   123

Part Four   129

Chapter 9: The New Humankind of the 5th Dimension   130
  – The Secret of the New Humankind's
    Ether Body   130
  – The Mysteries of 6 pairs of DNA Strands   131
  – The Smart Life Information System   132
  – The Connector to the Unseen World   133

Chapter 10: Chakra Restoration   135
  – A Chakra is a Relay Station of Information
    and Energy   135
  – The Essential Chakra called
    the "Danjeon"   136
  – The Principles of Transforming into a
    Different Dimension   138
  – A Semi-Etheric Body   139
  – The Life of the New Humankind   141

Chapter 11: Society and Culture after the Earth's Great
              Change   156
  – The Conditions for Passing through the
    Photon Belt   158
  – The Community Oriented Life — The
    Eco-Community   174

Part Five   179

Chapter 12: Some Cosmic Beings who were once on
              Earth   180
  – Socrates   180
  – Scott and Helen Nearing   188
  – A Saint of the Jungle; Albert Schweitzer   197
  – Mother Teresa; Mother of the Poor   205

– Mozart   215

– William Shakespeare   234

Chapter 13: A Beautiful Universe   246

– Characteristics of Planets and Stars
of Different Levels   246

Chapter 14: Cosmic Beings' Food, Clothing, Shelter
and their Life and Death   255

– Love and Marriage of Cosmic Beings   260

Chapter 15: The Year 2025 – The Future of the Earth   264

Chapter 16: Adapting to the Earth's Great Change
while overcoming the Crisis   270

– Individual, Corporate and National
Guidelines for Overcoming the Crisis   270

– Eco-Communities: Living for Co-Existence
and Awakening   274

– Break through Crises using Mankind's
Collective Unconscious   276

– The Energy of Love that Saves the Earth   278

Epilogue: 33 Ways of Practicing Love to Save
the Earth and its Family   282

Appendix: Introducing the Planets involved
in the Conversations   288

About Suseonjae   289

– Operation of Life Museums: Seon Culture
Experience Center   290

– Seon Culture Promotion and
Education Centers   290

About the Author   292

– Roar Sheppard   292

– Marlin   292

Prologue

I can't hide this anymore.

I'm going to be honest with you.

I speak to Cosmic Beings.

Helloooo? Are you still there? Are you ok?

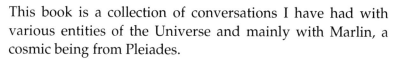

This book is a collection of conversations I have had with various entities of the Universe and mainly with Marlin, a cosmic being from Pleiades.

I know what you're thinking. Cosmic beings? Like, what do you mean? Aliens? But in fact cosmic beings are our friends, and they have been with us on the Earth since its beginning. They are not foreign to us; it's only us who have forgotten about them and the place where we come from in the Universe.

Ok, for some, this could be a bit hard to grasp, I know. Take a deep breath.

The purpose of this book is to bring our real family closer to us, which includes Mother Earth and all of her creatures and also our neighbours in the cosmos. Through this book, I hope to make them more familiar to us, if you will. Of course, this begs the question, how did we begin our contact with them and why are they suddenly talking with us anyway, at this specific moment in time?

Well, let me just give you a little bit of background about myself.

My name is Roar Sheppard and I am an American or at least I used to be, because now I rather see myself as just a citizen of the universe. I have spent the last 15 years living in South Korea. I wanted to know "who I am" and "where I come from" so badly since I was young, that at the age of 21, I just suddenly moved to the east, where I somehow thought I might find the answers. I ended up in South Korea.

I have spent over 8 years practicing breathing meditation. After spending years meditating and getting closer to nature, I discovered it was becoming possible to speak with plants, animals and even with the land itself. So when I heard there was a UFO hovering above South Korea's neighbour - Japan on the evening of the major tsunami in March 2011, it just felt natural for me to try to talk with the beings in the UFO.

I had never thought about cosmic beings much before, but suddenly I became interested in their feelings about this devastation to nature and human beings.

Unbelievably, I got connected to a tall, pony-tailed master of prophecy from Pleiades named Marlin.

After the initial shock, I asked why he had contacted me. His answer was simple. The first reason was because I knew how to do deep breathing and how to calm my mind and the second reason was that I already had a deep belief that other beings live in the Universe.

He told me that since many UFOs are coming to the Earth, it's a sign that the Earth is in imminent danger and the same way, the disappearance of the bee is another serious sign that Earth can no longer breathe. As their message is so urgent, he asked me to get their message out, but it's not just their message; it's a message from the entire Universe and all who live in it.

At first I hesitated to gather these conversations and make them into a book. The world will think I'm crazy. Who will believe this? But then again, when you read them, you will feel their truth. When you read them, you will feel their love.

And when you look at the present situation of the Earth, is there any doubt that we are in trouble?

What I realized was that all of us signed a contract before we were born on the Earth. We came here to evolve through a particular goal in this life. All of us. Also, the Earth is one of the most special planets throughout the entire Universe, as it's a school for evolution. Because of this, of course it's difficult to live here, but if we can get over the temptations of greed and selfishness, we can evolve endlessly to higher places.

Therefore the responsibility for the Earth lies with you. "The most precious being on the entire planet is you. It's so difficult to come to the Earth, but you came here. You came here because you are brave, because you wanted to evolve, because you are full of love." They wanted us to remember this.

The conversations about the photon belt and the crises to hit the Earth are true and terrifying, but we can survive only by awakening now. Through practicing love we can make it. At the end, it's a message of hope. After the dark night, a new day will dawn. For that reason, this book is a message of hope. There are large chapters about what the New Humankind will look like after the Earth evolves to the 5th dimension[1] and how society will be.

This is different from other channeling in that the conversations were done actively, not passively. In other words,

---

[1] The energy dimension of the Universe consists of the 1st through to the 10th dimensions. The Earth is standing by to ascend from 3rd dimension to 5th dimension. At present the oscillation frequency of the Earth is 3; the low frequency shows the planets is less evolved and has imbalances. In the future, when the Earth shifts to the 5th dimension after going through drastic purification process, the planet will show the same level of the cosmic beings who move freely between the material world and the spiritual world and send messages to the people of the earth. At that moment, human beings will recover all the 6 pairs of DNA (now they only have one pair of DNA) as they were originally created.

I could initiate the conversations at will. I think it was possible because I had done so many years of special breathing practice. Secondly, the main focus is not on the disaster of 2012, but on the power of love, the Earth's ascension and the hope of the New Humankind. Through love, care and selflessness, we will get over this period, like a butterfly removes its cocoon, all new and pure.

Finally, they tell us that small changes can make a big difference right now. If you reduce the garbage you throw away, and the next person reduces their meat intake, and the next person the amount of electricity in this way a new consciousness will spread around the Earth. You can find some clear guidelines about how to live well at the end of this book. But first, shall we hear their words directly?

Roar Sheppard

26 May 2011

Seoul, South Korea

Part I

Chapter 1

The Earth: a very Special Planet

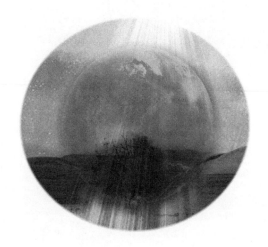

A Conversation with Mother Gaia

Tears of Mother Gaia

The Earth... Mother~

I would like to feel you. I want to converse with you.

Would you please be with us?

(All of a sudden I burst out crying.)

Why do tears well up in my eyes and sorrows rush into my heart?

(The Earth enters my body and fully fills up my heart.)

Because this is my present state......

(I have continuous sighs and deep breaths)

I feel so sad and frustrated that I can't even describe it.

Yes, I can also feel you.

As one of those who made you fall into this condition I am sorry to ask you, but would you tell me why your mind is this sore?

> I am so ill to the extent that I can't endure it. However, those who are ignorant of this pain account for the majority of people on the Earth. Why are they so indifferent even though I, who is the ground that they step on as well as the basis that provide the growth of all lives and food to eat, am suffering this badly? I am bruised and wounded by the indifference and despicable deeds of human beings. I feel like giving up any expectation or hope.

Oh, I am so sorry. I apologize for our ignorance, indifference and endlessly incessant selfish actions. Your pain is being passed on to me.

You are the Mother of the Earth. I would like to inform many people of your mind and condition through a conversation with you. Would you please allow me to do so?

> All right. I am skeptical whether people can change so easily, but why do I have to reject the efforts of people like you? If you can feel my mind and condition even a bit, please help me. Consequently this is the way to help all the people of the Earth because we share a common destiny.

I will. What should I call you?

> The Earth or the goddess of the Earth... Anything will do.

When I asked for this conversation, it sounded like a male voice. After that, I heard a female voice.

It is the expression of the Earth where male and female genders coexist. I am neither man nor woman.

Then why do people call you "Gaia," the mother goddess?

The Earth has a mother's attribute of embracing and nurturing all living creatures. That is why they call me Mother Earth.

May I call you Mother Gaia?

That's not bad. You may do so.

Abnormal weather changes or natural disasters are taking place everywhere now. We understand that they are signs of your ill condition. Now I am concerned for you. However, since many people are ignorant of your state and of the characteristics of nature, they don't know what is wrong and what to do to improve the situation. Even from now on, I am going to make an effort, so could you let me know about your condition and changes through conversation?

O.K.

How is your condition now?

The temperature inside the Earth is getting higher and the tectonic plates are moving. Eruption is possible anywhere anytime. Many places on the ground have been dug up and my skin is in too bad a condition to prevent the bad outside energies from coming in. Also, as the entire world has become metropolitan and industrialized, people have paved and covered much of the ground; I don't have much skin through which I can breathe. It is comparable to skin cancer.

Also, trees have been timbered so that it is not easy for me to regulate my temperature; I am exposed to hot weather or coldness just as I am. I am in my bare skin.

In addition, the sea is polluted; so in human terms, you can say I have got arteriosclerosis as my blood has become contaminated. Imagine your blood vessels were full of oil stains and sludge.

Even worse, cutting away mountains is the same as cutting away my bones and marrow. Can you imagine how painful it is? I don't have any sound body parts.

Oh, you are suffering so much. I am so sorry.

I don't know how I can even apologize. I don't have a word to say because I am one of those who have put you in this condition. As your pains are transferred to me, now I can understand what we have done to you. I can feel with my heart why the abnormal weather conditions and natural disasters happen on the Earth. As a matter of fact, human beings are only sensitive to their own benefits or pains.

Since last year, natural disasters occurred frequently. The climate is becoming stranger too. Earthquakes occur sporadically. The earthquakes which hit New Zealand and Japan were terrible.

The magnitude and intensity of earthquakes varied regionally but they occur continually. Do you have something to say about those?

When an earthquake occurs, it does not hit just one place. Many regions are designed to respond simultaneously. Earthquakes in New Zealand and Japan were unusually intensive and the plates of the Philippines, Korea, China and Myanmar are moving and are affected by the earthquakes.

The magnitude and intensity take place moderately and strongly in turn. Earthquakes or volcanic eruptions occur like a musical rhythm. Now it has a weak tempo, but when it gets strong again, any region can explode. When it explodes strongly, it is usually where volcanoes are located and it is highly likely to be along the circum-Pacific belt. Now plates are just warming up, like exercise. When it becomes time to start earnestly, the Earth will be hit by many earthquakes all at once like athletes on the starting line.

So, do you mean the earthquakes repeat faint or strong eruptions for some time and when it becomes time, they will hit the earth everywhere simultaneously?

Yes. Like in a rhythm, it goes forte, piano, forte, piano… and then it will blast all at once seriously. The heat inside the Earth and the downpour of universe energy are interlocked, so the Earth has no option but to begin its process of adjustment.

Then, is it possible to converse with you Gaia about the earthquakes and abnormal weather changes currently happening on the Earth?

People should show me their true hearts first. If the matter is really understood, feel sorry about me and approach with true concern so we can talk with each other; and we can discuss what's going to happen, and due to what cause. However, if you still have an egoistic mind to save only yourself, I would rather not. I replied to your request because I knew your mind.

Mother Gaia, I understand your mind. We will strive harder to enlighten ourselves about your sufferings and our indifference and egotism… I am so pleased to have this conversation with you today and I once again send you my heart of

regret. I will pray for you and all of us. I expect to see you again.

Your intention is good, so I also want to continue this conversation.

Is there anything more you wish to know?

We slept the night and woke up this morning. All creations on the Earth began their days. Do you also sleep at night like us?

I don't sleep. Even at night many creatures still have their activities. You forgot day and night on the Earth appear in an opposite way on the other side of the Earth. I watch many creations on the Earth living according to the rules and help them to maintain their lives. You human beings probably do not know how many things happen on the Earth. I know even minute activities about microbes because I am a mother who takes care of her children. Thus, I am very sensitive about even delicate movement or change. I am not dull or ignorant like humans are.

Humans are like the black sheep of the Earth family. What should we do because there are so many flocks of black sheep and they actually lead the Earth?

Yes, that is true. The Earth became like this because of them. They are like bullies. As those kids are not mature, they act rashly not knowing what will happen in the future.

Maybe you want to give them a hard time, right?

How did you know? As they bother people in the neighborhood and spoil its atmosphere, I want to give them a good scare. Then they might realize what they have done.

Gaia, as you talk about something serious in this way, I feel a bit lighter. How would you awaken mischievous humans before they commit something more serious?

First of all, I will tell them softly. If it doesn't work, I will show them what will happen several times, you know, as an example, so they can realize what true power is.

You said, you would tell them softly first. Can the message I am trying to send people be something you wish to tell?

Yes. You can tell them that as the Earth is in danger, please stop and change your current lifestyle. If you continue to live like this, you will provoke nemesis. Yet, not many people would understand it. Then they need to experience some natural disasters. People do not understand until they experience it. It looks difficult to change through words because the wall of the minds of people is very thick. They need a shock that can break their strong shells. In that way, natural disasters are not always bad. They make people feel pains and difficulties from them. Through natural disasters, they can look back on themselves.

In the recent case of Japan, I feel so sorry for them that their country became devastated by an earthquake in one day. Is Japan's case an example of what is going to happen to the Earth in the future? Does it mean the chance is high that such kind of disasters can take place in other countries?

Many people need to become more mature and grow their consciousness. When you face a life or death situation, you will have to reveal your level of consciousness. Humans evolve through those experiences and such extreme situations can play the role of very great teaching material for human evolution. When people come to understand this, it will help them grow their consciousness and evolve.

My heart is getting sore since I can feel the pain and heartbreak that each Japanese person feels.

Human emotions help you grow. That is why you need such suffering and pain. When you share others pains, this will also help you grow. It is love toward human beings. When that love covers the Earth, people will mature. Do not think too negatively about natural disasters or regard them as sad. In fact those are also things required for human growth.

Mother Gaia, thank you for your precious words today. Please take care of the Earth well. I know I can't dare to say this to you though.

I understand how you would feel.

The Relationship Between Gaia and our Collective Unconscious

(I can feel the expression of the Earth's condition through my body.)

Whenever I think of you, my body gets a bit twisted. And I can feel the heat gushing out of my mouth like a glaring volcanic eruption.

Also, I feel like shouting and blaming someone. And my heart is sore.

That is my condition. I expressed myself through you.

Now you can know I am also a living being? Although I tell people I am alive, they don't understand. So I expressed myself in such a way.

Mother Gaia, what is the difference between your consciousness and the collective unconscious of humankind?

The collective unconsciousness is the sum of the entire humankind's minds. It is the consciousness level of an ordinary human being. Gaia is the fundamental consciousness of the Earth. It is the consciousness of the Earth given by the Universe from the very beginning; it includes the operational system and originally equipped structure. That is the higher concept of the original consciousness that adjusts the Earth from the overall dimension. Figuratively speaking, a person has one's original nature[1] as well as unconsciousness. I am closer to the humans' original nature.

Then, how are you related to the collective unconscious? Do you mutually influence each other?

The collective unconscious is the consciousness that covers the original nature of the Earth. When the unconsciousness improves and its shell is finally cracked, the original consciousness of the Earth will be revealed; it is the same principle of the expansion or evolution of the human consciousness.

If the collective unconscious doesn't improve, the original "me" would always be shadowed by it. Therefore, by changing the collective unconscious of humankind, you can help me be revealed more the principle is that as the other consciousness becomes

---

[1] The original nature: One's true self, which resides internally and is ones friend for eternity. The everlasting love or the friend of eternity is in one's self, and through the meeting with the original nature, we come to know true love; that is, the love of the Universe. We can say the one who has met original nature is the person who knows and practices true love, the love of the Universe. We can see such cases from saints of high spirituality such as Buddha and Jesus.

integrated to the original consciousness, the original consciousness broadens. So when people change their minds and actions, I am pleased. See me as the Earth's consciousness residing deep inside.

Even now when I am conversing with you, my heart is sore as your pains are transmitted. I can feel the mind of a mother whose heart is bruised.

You are washing my pains with your energy. I thank you. I am grateful for your mind and energy.

I also thank you, Mother Gaia.

Gaia's Message to Everyone on the Earth

Were you sick because of radioactive rain yesterday?

Yes, I was. When it became afternoon, my body was strange. I felt sickness and my organs were uncomfortable.

I felt that the Earth is surely in danger.

How can I be fine? Radioactivity is fatal to many creations. This substance is so poisonous as to change even the DNA structure of many creatures. Animals, plants and the ocean around Japan are becoming seriously diseased; and that indicates human beings will soon be next.

A radiation accident in one country, Japan, affected the entire world. Then you can imagine how much I have been damaged so far because I am the Earth. The Chernobyl disaster still affects me. Once an ecosystem is damaged, it takes too much time to recover. Humans do not take it seriously and they are destroying the circulation system of nature for their own benefit and comfort.

Now you must change. If you do not seek co-existence with me and with nature, humans will no longer be protected. You can never know how patient I have been with you and how much effort I made to protect you. Children who do not care about the pains of their mother are not true children. Humans should grow now and understand the pains of their mother just a bit more. You should protect the Earth like you take care of your mother. I am so sad about this situation where I have to tell you myself. I am also ashamed, like a mother who has kids which have ill-treated her. Seek for a way to live together even now. I am giving this message not only to you but to all the people on the Earth.

Mother, I understand your profound intention. I will inform people of your message. What is the first thing that humans need to be concerned about in order to protect you?

First you should understand how the Earth is now. Pay attention to the message that the Earth is now giving. In order to change the world at large, many people need to make an effort at the same time. Even if it is just a small action, when many people participate in it, this will bring about a great change. Do not use disposable products, produce less garbage, grow even a single tree sincerely and so on – whatever it is, put one thing for the Earth into practice every day and become awakened; this is the condition I want from you.

The power of human thinking is larger than you expect, so when more and more people think that way, I will be influenced by the energy. Then my activity to purify myself will change too. A change in a human mind and a small change in a human action console me deeply; then I will probably change my mind-to live with you together. There is no such mother who does not pay attention to her children when her children make an effort to protect their mother. Show me such efforts and minds. Then I might change my mind too.

Purification activity is necessary at this time, however, when the mind and consciousness of humans are awakened and act with me, I can control it to a lower level and will only start purification activity where it needs to be purified. I am not sure if my message would appear to the hearts of many people but when more and more start believing in this message, the circumstance of humankind and the Earth will become advantageous. You know the power of single-mindedness, don't you?

Thanks for telling us how you think and feel. A change in one's mind even if it is small is more important than anything else. I am trying to produce less food-garbage nowadays. Let me look back at myself and do everything I can do in my daily living. Also I need to contemplate how I can effectively deliver your message to people.

Please you should first put those activities into practice and build networks with people who are doing similar activities like you so that the sphere and energy can be expanded. When more and more people gather, this becomes power. One of the ways to spread this message is to tell people about the Earth being in danger.

I see. I will try. Ah, I missed something. I wanted to ask you if radioactive rain still fall down for a while still.

Yes, it would. Rain can wash radioactivity in the air. It is a kind of purification activity of nature. Thus, you had better not go out in the rain. Sensitive people and some creatures respond to radioactivity more easily. Please avoid going out so that you don't get exposed to it.

Thank you. Mother Gaia, from your point of view, is there any region that requires severe purification? I am not sure if I am entitled to ask you this but I would like to be of help with our energy.

................(The Earth does not say anything.)

I apologize. I was not humble to have said so. Lastly, is there anything you wish for?

What is necessary now is change in the masses of people. Otherwise, my purification activity will become very severe. The change of humans is what I want and this is also a schedule of the Universe. It is not that I hope that only a few people change.

I understand your intention. I will try harder to inform people of your message. Thanks for the conversation.

Yes, I liked it too because I could tell you about my mind.

Chapter 2

A Conversation with the Collective Unconscious of Humanity

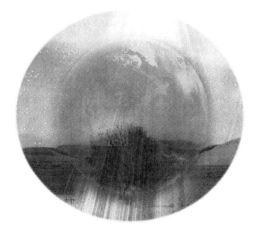

R: Roar (Communicator)

M: Marlin (Cosmic Being)

CU: The collective unconscious (*of all the human beings on the Earth*)

R: Mother Earth Gaia said that if the consciousness of the majority of humans doesn't change, the Earth will be put in danger. How can we change the direction? Humans' consciousness is so stubborn that it never seems to change despite the environmental movement. When can we change the minds of all 6 billion people? Fear... or frustration arises when I think about it.

M: Then, are you willing to meet it... the mind of 6 billion people?

R: What? Meeting the mind?

M: Let's meet the Collective Unconscious in person. Its not impossible. I told you that you can see it. So you can also read the ideas of the collective unconscious. I've never tried it before. Let's give it a try. This is the first time I've ever tried it myself.

R: I see. The collective unconscious... Is it talking to the unconsciousness of all 6 billion people?

M: Yes, it is. It's on the very bottom of the human consciousness. There are various types of groups, so there is collective unconsciousness that a family has, and there is another collective unconsciousness that a country has. Now who you should talk to is the collective unconsciousness of all humankind. Would you like to try it?

R: I will give it a try. By the way, will its consciousness change if I talk to it?

M: I have no idea because I've never tried it myself. Cosmic beings don't necessarily know everything. A higher dimension than the one where I belong has just opened up a way. Let me receive the wave[1] and make it possible for you to hear it. Regulate your breaths.

...

---

[1]Wave: The phenomenon where energy is transferred through the vibration of matter. At this moment, it is possible to transfer information as well as energy. For instance, supposing electricity is energy itself, the electric wave or radio wave is none other than a wave, and the wave enables radio broadcasting. All creations in the Universe communicate with one another through waves; one can even communicate with animals, plants, spiritual beings or cosmic beings using waves.

R: Marlin?

M: Start now. It looks like it will respond to you.

R: OK. Excuse me... Hello there...

CU: We see each other every day. Why are you feeling so awkward and shy? I'm the consciousness that dwells inside you. And I'm connected to everyone's consciousness. Take it easy. Just think that you are talking to yourself.

R: I see... Let me feel you for a moment. I would say it's complicated. I sense an image of a blond haired woman and the feeling of an arrogant man.

CU: Hmmmm. A white woman. That's the image that humankind seeks after. They have set the standard of beauty to white women, haven't they? And they also have a masculine tendency that wants to live a self-centered life. What made you talk to me directly like this? What do you want to know?

R: Ah.. I talked to a cosmic being, and he told me to appeal to the collective unconsciousness directly to prevent the crisis of the Earth. So I came to talk to you.
Marlin, is this image the right one, the one you saw?

M: It's not so different. It's that sort of image. Combination of the ideal type of person that people sexually pursue and human-centered thinking.

R: Hmm... That's beyond my expectation. You, collective unconsciousness, do you happen to know that a crisis is on its way to the Earth?

CU: How can I not know that? But I don't want to stop it. I'm satisfied with my present life. If the crisis comes, I will adapt myself to it, and wouldn't that be good enough? So many people are talking about the forth coming crisis, but I'm not positive.

R: Is it insensitivity? If so many things are happening in every corner of the Earth like this, some of them should be imprinted on unconsciousness. Don't you think?

CU: Look around yourself first. How much vinyl garbage are you making each day? Environmental issues are not the matter of unconsciousness but the matter of consciousness. Crisis? I knew it from the time of birth. Every day has been a crisis to me. Living day by day itself was a struggle for survival. Then, what difference is there between the forth coming crisis and living another day?

R: Is it correct that you live a new life day by day? But the crisis to come this time is a common crisis that all human-kind must go through. If we don't move together, we can never overcome it.

CU: I'm already aware that the crisis will come. But I have survived somehow whenever crises came. I will never disappear even if another one happens.

R: Marlin, it's not easy at all... When it comes to eloquence, I'm no match... Help me.

M: Roar, come on. You are talking to yourself. How can you be overpowered by his speech? Ha ha! Let me have a brief interview with him now. What I can do for you is to just help with understanding what's going on, though. Excuse me... Just for a second.

I'm Marlin from Pleiades. I came over to the Earth to cover a case and got this opportunity to see you. It's my honor. Can I ask you for an interview? On my planet quite a few people are interested in what's going on on the Earth. All are curious about dynamic life on the

Earth and wait for news every day. How about telling your stories? I think a lot of cosmic beings will like it.

CU: Is that so? That's interesting. You want to interview me! Let's try it. Ha ha ha!

M: How can I introduce you first? Is your name, "The Collective Unconscious"?

CU: I'm Atron. In each country I have a different name. They call me Atman, Idea and many other names, but I like Atron best.

M: I'd like to listen to your story - how you were born, how you grew up and what shaped you into present self and so on.

A: Why do you want to know such things?

CU: As I told you before, stories from the Earth are the most popular topic on my planet. Things happening on the Earth are rare even in the Universe.

A: Are they so unique in the Universe?

M: Sure. You know, when you look up at the night sky, the Universe is serene. We cosmic beings have our own lives on our planets, but we don't live such an emotional life as Earth humans. Things we go through in one thousand years, Earth humans go through in just ten years. Recently the speed is getting even faster.

A: Recently the consciousness in me has begun to be united. Each individual that has his or her own consciousness began to share each other's ideas. When I was first born… It was total darkness where I couldn't hear anything. I only thought about two things: my own survival and the discovery of who I am. There was nothing but the two.

M: When was it? When was the beginning?

A: I don't remember. It's been too long. I've existed much longer than I remember. When I became aware of myself, I was no longer a baby with parents. I was just "there" after having been born at some stage.

M: Maybe it was as if you were an amnesiac.

A: Maybe. I had no parents that one could call "mother". I just existed.

M: What did you do with the two thoughts of survival and finding out who you are?

A: I began looking out for myself. I thought I would have to survive until I found out who I was, where I was and what I was.

M: Were you all alone?

A: I was all alone. One day I saw a light on the surface. I heard conversation. Conversation was taking place on the layer of consciousness and I was watching it. I grew up while watching true mind hidden inside consciousness. You know, the true mind hidden in the emotion called love, the true mind sprouting inside the fence of family. I grew more and more while watching such things.

Consciousness is my nutrient. The true mind placed in the stream of consciousness brought me up. I wanted to survive and enjoy my life because I didn't want to feel lonely. Family and love were such a new energy to me who was alone.

M: Love... Then you grew up watching and feeling such love?

A: Well, you can say so but I needed more love. I was so lonely... Love was such a sweet life force to me.

M: So?

A: I started to intervene in humans' consciousness.

M: Intervening in humans' consciousness?

A: I told them what I wanted incessantly so that they would seek love incessantly. I asked them to create more love and new love. I kept sending them signals so that they would love consciously and keep loving. So many people fell in love and human consciousness gradually expanded. The number of individuals increased and various types of love sprouted. It was as spectacular as the Milky Way. I was happy.

M: Hmm…Atron, when you talk about love, I feel sadness rather than joy. Why is that?

A: Do you feel my emotion? That's very interesting.

M: I feel it well. I feel better than I see, and so does my friend here..

A: Oh, the guy typing hard next to you? Haha... I guess he does. When we first met, he felt my emotion very well.

M: That's why I asked you to converse with him. Although he asked me to talk to you for him, saying he's not an eloquent speaker, he sympathizes with others well.

A: Well, I will keep an eye on you. I will see how much you can feel.

M: Then, let me continue. Why do I feel sadness in you?

A: I'm not content with just watching. There are countless stars in the sky but nothing is mine. I want to feel warmth right next to me. That is why… Although

I intervene in human consciousness, I can only see and feel it. It's not next to me though.

M: I see. Can I define it as loneliness?

A: You know, I don't like the word so much - "Loneliness". Let's call it a day. I want to stop here today.

(Atron fades out from consciousness)

M: That is how Atron is. It's his feeling at that time rather than his present situation. He feels as if he were left alone in the Universe... Let's keep talking to him and continue the conversation. Maybe there will be progress.

R: All right... It was like I was watching myself from next to me. You know, no matter how much I desire love, I still feel so lonely. That's ironic.

M: I see. That's the mystery of the Earth we cannot understand.

I got to know that the consciousness delivers energy to the unconscious. So let me think about how to change human consciousness.

Human Consciousness has lost its Rudder

R: Do you remember? We are Marlin and Roar, the ones you spoke to last time.

A: Why did you come again?

R: I came here because I just wanted to see you. I got to know you so I was wondering how you have been.

A: I know to some extent what's going on in your consciousness. Do you want to tell me there is not much time remaining? Probably. All people say we don't have enough time. Yet, I am still alive today. Don't try to persuade me in a clumsy way.

R: Hmm... Persuading you? Well, I wouldn't say I have no such an intention, but today I came here just to learn about you. It's an extension of the previous interview.

A: OK, go ahead. Perhaps I need to talk to your cosmic being friend? I don't feel anything new from you.

R: Ha ha... I see. Then Marlin, please!

M: Wow! How have you been? It's been a week or so and you haven't changed at all.

A: Why do I have to change?

M: Japan was hit by an earthquake a few days ago. It was the 3rd one. Then, don't you feel you should consider changing now?

A : ... …

M: You were a bit shocked, weren't you?

A: Yes. It was the first time I've seen so many people die at once. It all happened in a very short time.

M: Didn't you go through a similar experience when atomic bombs were dropped in Japan?

A: That was a part of human affairs. There was a clear reason. However, this tsunami was not something we could expect or prepare for. I am getting scared.

M: Japan has been hit by earthquakes often, so it is well prepared for this natural disaster, isn't it? It's surely prepared for earthquakes and people know how to deal with this natural disaster.

A: Yes, that's why I am wondering more this time. The Japanese usually prepare so well for it, even to a meticulous degree. But they are swayed and scared. I feel it is dangerous now.

M: Atron, I have been watching the history of the Earth. I haven't watched it everyday, but when an important moment comes to the Earth, many disasters occurred. Can I call it a turning point? At these turning points, things changed and history progressed forward little by little. That's the history of humanity I watched. You know it is like a bamboo joint. When humans passed by one joint, they always went through a rite of passage like that.

A: Does it look like a rite of passage? Is that so?

M: Yes, it is a rite of passage. How you deal with this change will decide your future.

A : ... ...

M: Are you getting a little more interested in it?

A: Hmm...You are a good speaker. Please continue.

M: O.K. Atron. How do you like your life on Earth? You are in charge of the unconsciousness, and your counterpart is consciousness. Is there a difference between the two?

A: Well, I guess you should not see them that way. Consciousness is an illusion that I make. I am the prototype and there are phenomena. When a phenomenon and I meet each other, a variety of reactions appear. That is consciousness. Therefore the two are not different things. To speak more easily, I am the mind, while gestures and language are consciousness.

M: Is there such a thing as the collective consciousness too? I don't think each individual consciousness of 6 billion people all comes from you, Atron.

A: Hahaha! You underestimate me. Each consciousness arises from me. I knew already you would come to me like this. There were some people who came and talked to me before. We had a lot of conversations and they got a better understanding of what a human being is. However, I cannot control everything of humans. I am the prototypical consciousness underneath each individual's consciousness. I am also the expression of someone else.

M: Do you know who that is?

A: Yes, I do. It is God or original nature. There are so many different names for that. I feel it and follow its voice. But, over half my personality is against it. The will to survive, that is the other half of myself. I want to live. I need more proliferation. We have to increase population through more proliferation. I can attain my goal when I reproduce more individuals.

M: What is it? What is the goal? The proliferation of humankind? Do you feel fine just as long as you can reproduce more humans?

A: No. Producing individuals is my first goal. When many individuals are born, I can do many things. Many cultural things and new events take place. Now I am a bit tired. Always the same old story. Nothing is new. Well, it seems that something progressed a great deal but then it became stagnant. Although there is a slight difference, all are really the same daily routines. My will to proliferate is diminishing little by little.

M: A new event that will even threaten your survival is coming. As observed in the Universe, current human activities have reached the level of danger. Isn't this new?

A: Well, it is not a big deal that a couple of people die. Even now many people are dying. I too will die someday. When I am gone, that's it.

M: When a human dies, the body is gone but the consciousness moves to another dimension. You can be born in the Universe or on the Earth again. I don't think it is just a matter of helpless death.

A: I know another dimension exists. Isn't that a place where you go when you die? I don't understand what you want to talk about.

M: Roar, Atron seems to lose his direction. Atron forgot about the direction called evolution. If the direction to go forward is not given clearly, it seems he would stay in that state.

R: I see. The purpose of life doesn't look clear. Is that how humans feel now?

M: Not completely, but it is true that it reflects the state of most humans. Let me continue a bit more. Atron, the current humankind is in the 3rd dimension. They have to get over the forth coming crisis well and move on to a higher dimension. You will have a new start. You won't live like you do now but will live in the Universe becoming one with each other. You have so many things to learn before that day.

A: Even that's not new to me. I know it already. When the time comes, I will respond to it then.

M: Atron, why do you proliferate on the Earth?

A: I would like to reproduce many individuals. Many people can be born. Then humankind develops. And many interesting events occur when they collide with one another.

M: Development in which direction? The material civilization has reached its peak, hasn't it?

A: Well, I haven't been there yet, so I don't agree with you on the words "peak". Maybe there is something above that.

M: The next civilization is the one in which the mind and material evolve together. Many planets in the Universe went through the same process as the current Earth. Also, the Earth has reached a moment now when it will change now. It is a kind of entrance exam. The way to solve this is to throw out your desire for material gain, and all become aware that the Earth, nature and humans are one family. Only then can you realize that the Earth and the Earth's family are one living creature. With that power, you can create a new civilization. You look so bored and tired, and if you stay like that, you can never pass the exam.

A: Well, it doesn't sound so persuasive. It cannot change my behavior. I am playing my role well enough now. When the exam comes, I can deal with it somehow. Humankind has always been living that way.

M: This test won't be so easy. Many planets in the Universe are now watching the Earth. It is that difficult. With the current level of awareness, you will suffer from tremendous pain.

A: As long as I and my surroundings are all right, everything is fine. Well, pain is something I have to undergo, right? If each one lives his life where he is, all is O.K.

M: Roar, we'd better stop here today. It is harder than I expected.

R: I understand. I can see the overall disposition.

M: Yes. Arrange the conversation and let's discuss this again. Atron, thanks for the conversation. I would like to talk to you more. Can we have a conversation again next time?

A: Yes. Next time, please come to me with more refreshing issues. I would like to hear more of new stories in the Universe.

M: Yes. I will bring more interesting stories next time. That is my specialty. See you next time.

A: ....

R: Marlin, I felt as if I were talking to a wall.

M: Yes. As a matter of fact, unconsciousness does not change so easily. This was the first time I talked to it myself, but the communication didn't go well. I guess I need to understand it more. And, I already knew the inner human mind would be like that.

R: Yes. When I listened to his answer, I felt a prick at my conscience as if that was how I thought. I don't think we can work it out overnight.

M: That is reality. If one said that collective unconscious could change in a day, it would be fiction. We don't have much time, but we have to talk to him as often as possible and induce change. Of course, both talking to the unconsciousness directly and conscious actions have to be made together. When consciousness changes one by one, that is meant to affect unconsciousness too. So be well-aware of that fact and make an effort.

R: Thank you, Marlin.
Maybe we can find out how to direct the future conversations.

M: Ok. You got a bit of a clue, didn't you?

R: Yes, I did. I will keep telling him about the crisis and help to make him do even small things. And I will have to appeal to consciousness continuously so that it can see the overall picture.

M: Exactly. Opening his consciousness and expanding his horizon is necessary. His understanding of environment or ecology is limited. It looks very necessary to explain it for his better understanding.

Chapter 3

The "Earth" that Cosmic Beings Speak of

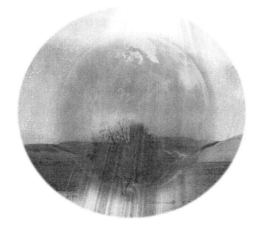

The Earth: a very Special Planet

Would you please explain me to about why you contacted us, the Earth people?

As you may know by watching the news, the Earth is now heading toward a precarious situation. Due to thoughtless development that doesn't consider the environment, the Earth is sick.

If this situation goes on, you Earth people, a group sharing a common destiny with the Earth, cannot remain safe, either. We are trying to inform you of the forthcoming crisis and would like to provide you with the necessary information and aid in order to help you steer your direction to saving the Earth.

What specific help can you give us?

Rather than telling you "This is it", we can give you
the right help from our dimension depending on the
situation.

**I understand. By the way I have a question. From the
viewpoint of development level of civilization, planets such
as Sirius or Pleiades must be far more advanced than the
Earth. What is the reason you are interested in the Earth?**

The level of a civilization itself cannot be a criterion by
which to measure the value of a planet. That is not the
standpoint of the whole Universe. It's as if on the Earth
the worth of a person is not determined by whether he
is rich or whether he has a high status or not. This is
the reason why we are interested in the Earth; with
respect to its value, the Earth is known as one of the
most important and rare planets in the Universe.

**Is that so? Why do they say that the value of the Earth is
high? It must be common to think that the value of a planet
with more developed technologies in either mental or
material areas is higher.**

The value from the standpoint of the Universe is
decided by what role you are playing in the Universe,
rather than how much of a developed state you are in.
It is the same principle as the value of a person being
decided by how much positive influence he has on
those around him, rather than by how high a status
he holds or how rich he is. The Earth was created to
perform an enormously positive role in the Universe
by its nature.

This planet provides an environment where a soul can
achieve a tremendous spiritual growth within a short
period of time. The density of energy is very high

and the kinds of the energy also vary; therefore the combination and clash between those different energies gives birth to enormously various environments. I called it energy, but to express it in the way of the Earth, it is countless emotions, varied personalities and varied conditions. You experience myriad things in such circumstances and through those experiences your soul grows.

An evolved planet cannot offer that sort of condition for the growth of a soul. It seems like a soul can grow fast if he has plenty of time and a good environment, but that's not the case. The growth of a soul is not achieved only because he has a lot of time to see and hear so many things. It can come about when hardship or conflict is given like the circumstances on the Earth and he eventually overcomes it.

It sounds like you put the conventional saying "Good rain and storms ripen crops" in the Universe's way. If so, why does only the Earth have such a good condition? Wouldn't it be better if there were many such planets?

That's a good question. The amount of rain and storms should be proper for crops to ripen. The environment of the Earth is not only appropriate as you can see. There are so many various programs in which you can experience literally from heaven to hell. It is not that all people evolve through the programs.

There are so many people going in the negative direction by being hurt, suffering, belittling themselves and being corrupted in the face of temptation, hardship and conflicts that they should have overcome in order to grow. The current Earth is at a point where the negative trend is gaining momentum and so it is getting dangerous.

When there are only one or two planets with this complexity, it is positive because it gives stimulation to the universe around it and plays a role as a school for the souls who want to evolve fast. But if there were many such planets, it plays a role to reverse the stability of the Universe. In the medieval times each royal court had a clown, didn't it? The clown was necessary to brighten the atmosphere, but suppose there were too many such people. When all of them shout and act at the same time, it would be total chaos.

It is so amazing that the Earth is a planet with such a special value even in the Universe. Now I can understand the reason why cosmic beings pay attention to the Earth more and more.

On the Earth, people regard the word "a special being" to apply to some and not others; however in fact all of those on the Earth probably belong to the group called "special beings". That is because the Earth is such a special planet and all the living beings on this special planet are having such special experiences.

The Purpose of the Earth's Creation

Then, I am curious about how this "special" planet where I live was created. How was the Earth created?

We can say that it is true that the Universe was created by a collision of meteors after the Big Bang. Nevertheless, it is so only when we view the event from the physical and Earth dimensional eye since we can't explain everything by dividing, analyzing, colliding and exploding. Just as when we create something, we make it after thinking about its usage, we need to know with what purpose the Universe created it.

Then, for what purpose was the Earth created?

It is a school. The Earth was granted the role of being a school. The curriculum is what you discover about your true self through numerous "experiences" and through the application of your free will to them. One is born after having one's existing memories erased. People who are studying in the school, planet Earth, have to realize all the problems they encounter now and the process of finding out one's self while sorting out the problems is the course that evolves them quickly.

Did the Earth begin to play the role of a school from the very moment of its creation?

No. The Earth prepared its foundation as a school as it evolved through various methods over a long time. That is to say, its program was arranged by the Creator, but the Earth was not ready to operate the program from the beginning. It is like the Earth had to first prepare itself to accommodate its students.

In terms of the human body, the Earth is an organism, as is the Universe; and each planet, star or galaxy has its own role as a certain part. Accordingly, the evolution of a planet brings about that of another planet or star simultaneously whereas the regression of a planet also causes that of another planet; so from the standpoint of the Universe it is such a loss.

The Earth is a quick-training planet[1]; so many planets dispatch their people to the Earth with special missions.

---

[1] The Earth is the planet where one can accomplish enormous evolution in a short time and tests with high level of difficulty are provided. From the standpoint of human beings, it can be viewed partly as a gambling house, but since all the things are operating the right way, there is no room for flukes.

Not just anyone can come to the Earth[2] even if they wish to and one can't just leave the Earth easily as one pleases.

From the viewpoint of the Universe, all the planets and stars can be brothers to one another; but since there are few planets where so many races are living, mixed together, we can say there is no planet that is not a brother to the Earth. In this sense, we cosmic beings are even more concerned about the Earth.

What does it mean when you say that cosmic beings perform their roles on the Earth well and return to their home planets?

It is the same as graduating from a top class university and contributing to your country. However, evolved cosmic beings are not working in that way according to the concept of possession where they use their talent for their own good, but they are doing so because they know that taking care of the evolution of their planet and the Universe is consequently good for oneself and everyone. If they come back after successfully completing their roles, they can give support to delegates who come after them. Also, those who come back successfully can work for the evolution of the planets; therefore the level of the planets can be upgraded, thanks to them.

One of the greatest achievements through the experience on the Earth is that one can learn about

---

[2] Planets that can transmit their waves to distant planets are rare, since their spiritual civilizations are highly developed, even if their material civilization is of a low level, and the Earth is one such planet. Planets that have attained a high level of civilization are aware of the existence of the Earth. It is that the planet has harmonized with a million kinds of energy and this energy condition is not common even in the Universe. These planets only appear one in 600 galaxies.

various kinds of energy; through the energies, one can learn about the energy of the Universe

Energy is that important. By the way, how do you utilize your knowledge about the energies you acquired on the Earth?

In energy, the infinite information of the Universe is hidden. One makes slow evolution since he/she doesn't know about the various kinds of energy. If one acquires new energy, it is as if the learner gets information about another dimension through the new learning and can upgrade their level.

Life on the Earth as a physical space never goes smoothly. What you see or hear in the limited world paralyzes the original human senses. Because of that, you miss what you are supposed to pursue and what is most important.

Then, what would be important things we shouldn't miss?

OK. To begin with let me tell you about the evolution of a soul. You think cosmic beings are even more evolved than humanity because they have developed civilization, science and technology, but that is half correct and half wrong. The essence is about souls contained inside the bodies of humanity on a planet. I've once told you that the development phase of a soul is the barometer of value standard from the standpoint of the Universe.

Cosmic beings look like more evolved human races because they have much higher I.Q. and more abilities, but that doesn't necessarily mean that they have high level of soul. It's just because they are under such conditions. It can be compared to the difference between an airplane pilot and a bike rider. It's not that the airplane pilot can travel around the world faster because the level of his soul is higher.

In the Universe, even in the same space there are various dimensions from the 1st dimension to the 10th dimension. Here, "dimension" also signifies the existing forms of energy. The Earth is a planet of the 3rd dimension that exists as matter, and matter imposes a tremendous load on the soul.

Because the soul, a being of high dimension dwells in the body of the 3rd dimension, that imbalance interlinked with birth-aging-disease-death provides souls with all kinds of life study. Those are also expressed as various programs for the evolution of the soul.

Confined in the body of the 3rd dimension, all you see, hear and feel are also limited to the 3rd dimension, and it makes human ability look limited. But that is because a human being temporarily has a heavy load while living on the Earth. If he frees himself from his body through training in this environment, he can achieve enormous growth. On the other hand there is another case where he gives in to the environment and regresses, so the Earth is a school with a strong nature of adventure.

Listening to what you said, I had an idea. Why were we Earthlings born on this complex planet and why have we been suffering? We could have been born on other planets, so is it just because we had a bad luck draw?

Hahaha! To draw a conclusion first, those who were born on the Earth at this age have had extremely good luck. It is a long story if I tell you all the reasons. Let me tell you a few of them. You are wondering "Why was I born on the Earth and have to live a difficult life like this?", but the difficult life usually lasts no more than 80 years.

Compared to the age of your soul that has lived tens of thousands of years or even millions of years, that is as short as one flash of lightning. Depending on how you spend the time period at this school, you can accomplish incredible progress even in one lifetime. To achieve such progress it may take other souls in the Universe millions of years, even tens of millions of years. What's important is whether you know the fact and make good use of it, or whether you just regress without knowing it and are swept by circumstances around you.

Also, a considerable number of people who live on the Earth were born according to their own free will. It's just that they don't remember why they were born on the Earth because the learning program of the Earth has such a structure that you forget your previous memory completely and have to seek for your original self. If you just make it to find your lost original memory, even that is considered as a big success. A good number of people are swept away by the environment and cannot discover their original self, which eventually makes them bound to the Earth. That is described as reincarnation.

To make a long story short, so many human races in the Universe are born on the Earth for rapid evolution. If they succeed, they evolve above their original positions. If they fail, they are re-born continuously until they find their original self, being bound by reincarnation on the Earth and not being able to return.

"If you do well, you hit the jackpot. If you don't, you go bankrupt and can't even go back home." It sounds more like a gambling place rather than a school.

You may see it that way. You bet your original self. You can say the prize is the evolution which shortens time by hundreds of thousands of years - up to even tens of millions of years. But there is one reason we don't call the Earth a gambling place. That is because your own effort is the most crucial condition. Luck is also a big factor, of course.

The Earth's People are Foreign Students from other Planets

If so, all the human races living on the Earth now are from the Universe?

Even though there are many people on Earth who are native to the Earth naturally for sure, a larger number of humans are from the Universe and have their own home planets.

We can say that most of them are transplanted from the Universe because of some intention. The greatest purpose of the transplantation is to receive the waves of the planets where the transplanted beings have originated from. In this process, it is not that the Earth only receives waves from those planets, but that the waves of the Earth are transferred to them and they can take advantage of the waves as their energy source because various kinds of energy which are emitted from the Earth can be a power source for other planets. Numerous kinds of energy are latent on the Earth, and the power generated from the interaction of those energies transmits to other places in need of it. All of this process is possible through waves.

You may now understand that waves are just the means for telepathic communication with me; however the power of waves is way more formidable. To deliver waves effectively as well as to receive the waves of a planet well, they use the method of transplanting souls on the Earth and arranging for them to be born there. You can regard it similar to changing into clothes that fit you in a fitting room.

In your case too, you also borrowed the physical body of the Earth's people. There are two kinds in such cases: the former is a case where one gets permission to be born on the Earth and chooses a body with suitable DNA while standing by as a soul; this is only allowed for high level of souls. The latter is changing a person's soul in some special cases.

All of these are possible only when they get permission from the Earth. Here the "permission of the Earth" is close to going through passport control and customs when you go traveling to other countries. Also, before this process the planet that wants transplantation of a soul evaluates the soul first. It is not that they send anyone randomly. We can see it a kind of dispatch. Nevertheless, due to the oblivion program[3] of the Earth, people forget about the fact completely and are living too much of an earthly life.

---

[3] The Earth is a planet created as a school for experience. Once one is born on the Earth with a physical body, he/she can't come back until they complete their course of study. In this course people have to begin from the bottom state, giving up what they have accumulated such as knowledge or memory. In such a planet, there is a unique rule called 'reincarnation' and until one realizes his own path, one will lead his life in oblivion of his true self. The chance of losing everything one has accumulated is so high that huge resolution is required to enter this course; but the earning after the success in the course is also great.

That is to say, the intrinsic attributes of the Earth are: wanting to have more to win and to dominate others. The reason the Earth is a school is because it offers so many experiences to those humans who were born on the planet. The experiences are like growth rings for souls. A myriad of growth rings are engraved in the soul, experiences are like inner property, which manifests as wisdom.

This wisdom makes a positive contribution to the development of the Universe. It's not that having as many experiences as possible unconditionally is good. You should learn through the experiences. Like a saying which goes "Failure is but the threshold of success", you should extract soul enriching nutrients from your experiences.

If you understand what I said, you get to focus on your inner side to find your original self and live your life with the purpose of developing your spirituality, rather than living an external, material life. Letting you know this fact is also the purpose of our contact with the Earth's people. It's a very simple principle, but whether you know it or not can be compared to choosing which branch of a road to take on the crossroads of heaven and hell. The reason I contacted you is because I wanted you to know and spread this.

It's like telling someone "In reality you were the princess of the kingdom X who just lost all her memory. Be awake and recover the dignity of a princess."

Right. You must realize how much of a precious being you were in your original self. When you are so worn out by the hardship of life, how touching would it be if you could recover the original noble character you had before you came to the Earth? You may even shed tears. You should have a mind of conveying that deep impression to others.

Dimensional Ascension: the Planned Schedule for the Earth

Can I ask you about the goddess of the Earth, "Gaia"?

It would be easier to understand if you regard Gaia as the entity of the collective intention that the Creator's intention left at the time of the Earth's creation in the form of an energy. When we compare it to a human, it falls under yeong[4]. So, it has its own will. It came into existence together with materials and is governing itself.

It is called "Mother" or "goddess" because it is the generator that gave birth to all animate and inanimate beings on the Earth. However, the Earth, which was created as an educational planet and the program called reincarnation is applied to, consists of the 3rd dimension, the visible material world and the 4th dimension, the unseen, spiritual world; and it is not that Gaia makes all the decisions regarding things on the Earth by itself.

For this, higher dimensions get involved in the decisions from the bigger frame. Probably we can see that as the role of the original nature of the Universe, that is a father; it falls under yeong (soul). To sum up, if we say Enlightenment of all creations on the Earth is the returning process by realizing the gratitude for the mother Earth and

---

[4]A yeong (soul) is one's true nature of the Universe before it becomes incarnated through his/her birth. While a fetus is growing in a body, one's soul stands by in the Universe and enters the body when the fetus is delivered. At this moment a yeong is connected and enters in the body; it is a physiological entity in charge of expressing one's intention regarding instinct. A person's mentality is formed by the combination of a soul and a yeong. A soul is in charge of high dimensional thinking and sentiments while a yeong is in charge of sentiment in terms of instinct.

understanding the profound will of the father Universe, that would be an appropriate figure of speech.

Abnormal phenomena happening on the Earth, such as unusual climate change, are operated by Gaia, that is the intentional entity, on her own to a certain extent, but at the critical moments, the Universe of another dimension gets involved, and now is also one of those moments.

Up till now, cosmic beings' intervention was allowed by Gaia; that is, the collective intention of the Earth and reacts together. But now, the contrary, is the decisive moment when the Universe involves itself firsthand and cosmic beings can intervene only with strict permission. Physically, it is the time when the Earth passes through the photon belt [5]for a dimension leap.

For the Earth to maintain its homeostasis as a planet of animate beings, it is meant to recharge itself with energy through the creative destruction of materials as if plowing a field. Especially, the system, represented as the Earth's magnetic field has the role of keeping the balance by weaving the material forms of the Earth's energy, that is Ji-su-hwa-pung (the 4 basic elements that forms the material world) like a grid by unifying the directions of energy into one.

---

[5] The photon belt is a gigantic area of photons containing massive photon energy that assumes the shape of a doughnut. The photon energy is one of the most innocent kinds of energy in the Universe and it is so minute and powerful that it can penetrate any thing or place in the Universe. Its surface is covered by cosmic rays, so they get rid of and cleanse unnecessary stuff. The earth is now entering the photon belt and to pass through it, a purified body and mind is required. If a person doesn't empty himself enough or is not familiar with universe energy, he can't endure the light and may feel enormous confusion.

I know that the things earthman did before will bring such excessive consequences, and I feel disheartened. Is there any way to restore the Earth to be like it used to be?

There would be a difference in the degree, but it is a massive flow stream of the Earth, which cannot be reversed. The only difference is how strongly it will arise depending on how many mistakes human beings committed.

You mean that this is the thing which inevitably has to come?

Yes, that's right. That has some connection with the stream flow of history, which has been repeated on other evolved planets. The history of planets generally follows the flow stream: Phase 1: spiritual civilization, Phase 2: material civilization and Phase 3: spiritual civilization based on material civilization.

When we view the final goal as human evolution, isn't it possible to accomplish perfect evolution from the Phase 1: spiritual civilization? Do they necessarily have to undergo the process of experiencing the abuses of material civilization?

The evolution of human beings is not accomplished merely through spirit. If so, there would not be a reason why the Earth, the material 3rd dimensional planet should be a training planet, would it? All sorts of temptations represented as materials are dangerous things, but actually it is the essence of study on the Earth. In other words, all kinds of tests and teaching materials for tests and studies that foster human beings can be obtained, through the development of materials.

That is a reasonable explanation.

Yes. When materials are endowed to the consciousness that has grown to a basic level, their thinking develops even higher. When we classify yeong-seong (spirit-nature; that is spirituality) into the power of yeong[6] (spirit; the most similar concept is intelligence quotient) and the power of nature (the original nature; the will to live a righteous life), through methods of taking advantage of materials, their power of yeong, that is their intelligence develops a lot. So to speak, just as if one can develop his/her intelligence by often solving puzzles, pondering on how to make money can become the positive process to improve one's power of thinking.

However, when the material civilization is developed as such, what will mainly develop is the power of spirit from yeong-seong (spirituality). To tell you in an easy way, areas related to thinking and intelligence develop while the power of nature, that is conscience or morality is blinded by materials; going through such process is an inevitable consequence.

For this reason, on other planets, when material civilization is developed, the process that leads to the collision and war can almost be considered to be a compulsory course. After going through that process, awakening will follow. It is the awakening about the fact that the development of the intelligence will only lead to mutual destruction. Through such pain by the collision, people come to seek for the development of the power of nature, which is the better value.

---

[6] The power of yeong is close to IQ (intelligence quotient); it signifies the ability to attain high ranks in work places and acquire financial success and fame. On the contrary the power of seong (the original nature) means a will to live a righteous life. When only one's power of yeong is highly developed while having poor power of seong, he/she would vainly pursue wealth, worldly power or fame. By combining the yeong and seong, it is called yeong-seong (spirit-nature; ie, spirituality). We can say upgrading and evolving one's spirituality is the most brilliant achievement in one's life after being born as a human being.

What is the concrete meaning of "the development of the power of nature"?

It refers to the degree of a soul's becoming one with the Universe. How close one is to the original nature or the original state of the Universe is the true value. The collision that I mentioned earlier is made in the realm of instinct. The awakening to return to the original nature, that is the original state of the Universe arises at the point of the extremity of the material civilization. If such an awakening level is not high enough, they are designed to perish.

That is to say, when the material civilization reaches its end point, people must choose between two alternatives; either to perish, or to choose the even development of spirituality to overcome the crisis of civilization?

Is it a matter of course to choose the latter?

It is a matter of course, but it is the reality that something of course doesn't work out as one wishes. Also, you don't even behave naturally in every facet of your life, do you? The human race is the same as well. They think that they naturally have to do that, but they have the momentum with which they have behaved before. That momentum is egotism. If people don't overcome this egotism, the civilization results in collapse.

If they develop the power of nature to get over egotism, that is, if they adopt spiritual civilization, a new epoch opens. Namely, Phase 3: spiritual civilization based on material civilization will open. It is the stage where both sides: mind and materials are not biased to any side but form harmony and create a synergetic effect. In this state, the planet can bring about the escalation of its grade because the level of the overall members makes a leap.

Do you mean that the dimensional ascension of the Earth is the planned project of the Universe?

Yes, it is. Previous humankinds who have lived on the Earth before the current humankind or evolved cosmic beings from other planets went through the process of evolution, but it happened step by step. It is the first case throughout the history of the Universe that a planet of the 3rd dimension like the Earth will ascend to the 5th dimension. The great change of the Earth to take place this time can be seen as the total evaluation regarding the evolution of people as well as all living beings who have lived on the Earth. All the people who now live on the Earth knew before that this change was coming, and chose to be born here. They are not aware of this fact now, because their memory about their previous lives is erased when they come to the Earth, but for sure it is true.

The Role of the Earth's People after the Ascension

If human beings keep regressing against the direction of evolution, as we do now, I am afraid of what will happen in the future. As our conversation goes on, it occurred to me that human beings are just a part of the numerous living beings on the Earth.

You are right. We are conversing with you for the awakening of human beings, but this is not only for the sake of humans. This is the stage where we all awaken others and also get awakened, and in the meantime we prepare for the dimensional shift together.

Can we reach the new dimension all together?

Yes, it is possible. That is because human beings are not the only beings on the Earth.

At the moment when the Earth passes through the photon belt, it signifies that all living creatures are newly born. Beings that can pass through the photon belt will be newly born as those of the new dimension.

Then, what do animals and plants need to do for the changing period?

That is the resolution of karma with which they entangled and cycled in the chain of the reincarnation. In the survival method in the law of the jungle that exists on the Earth, karma is created. In the case of human beings, the karmic debts can be heavier than those of other creatures. However, there can be difference in degree, but every being has karma. Only when all cast off the karma, can the Earth shift to another dimension.

People commit evil deeds even though they know the deeds are not right and go against reasons; they have to repent these sins and get awakened true-heartedly. In addition, resolving the deep-rooted grudges toward human beings that other living creatures hold can also be a good way of clearing the karma.

Consequently many things are up to human beings.

Yes. Humans are the beginning of all of these karmic debts, so if people clear the debts away, other beings will also naturally resolve theirs. Now the time has been delayed for too long. You don't have time.

You should recognize the fact that before you were born on the Earth, you were yearning for evolution in the Universe. Even if you were born with all things forgotten, you have to awaken at least that single memory by all means.

You, who originally existed as pure and innocent souls in the Universe chose the course of the Earth and came here to exist as a part of the Universe by evolving yourself further. You didn't visit this planet to reside permanently but you chose a school from which it is hard to graduate, in order to grow into a more evolved being by completing the course of the Earth.

You should become aware that your physical form in the material realm of the 3rd dimension is not all there is, but is just a part. By having your body as a tool, cultivating your soul to be pure and beautiful is the sole purpose of being born on the Earth. Only when you accomplish that purpose, can you feel all your inner longing fulfilled and only then can you have crowning contentment. Only then can you become qualified as a universal citizen who is a part of the Universe and you can complete the calling[7] you came to this special planet Earth for at this special period.

We cosmic beings hope for the awakening of you Earth people. We are waiting for the day when your souls will wake up and recover consciousness of the Universe, and travel around the Universe with us as fellow universe citizens.

---

[7] It is the task or work granted by the Universe; that is carrying out one's own work in one's position.

Part 2

Chapter 4

The Earth's Dimension Ascension and the Photon Belt

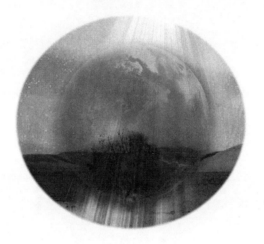

The Earth of the 5ᵗʰ Dimension... Will it be Possible?

Is the Earth scheduled for a dimensional ascension?

Up until now the Earth, which has been composed of the 3rd dimensional material world and the 4th dimensional realm of souls, operated in the Universe as a school with a high level of difficulty where living beings can make fast evolution through the system of reincarnation. Up till now the people on the Earth were born with an unbalanced physical body and soul constrained in three dimensional space and time. However, in the process of overcoming those restrictions and adapting to the environment and through experiencing numerous conflicts and reconciliation, their consciousness has been able to accomplish a high level of evolution. But from now on according to the plan of the Universe and the Earth, it is time for the Earth to finish its role as a school and return as a member of the Universe by evolving into a planet of the 5th dimension.

By the way, how can the Earth evolve into a 5th dimensional planet? Won't cosmic beings of other planets relocate to the Earth to reside here replacing the current humankind instead?

That is not it, so don't worry. It was prearranged from the moment of the Earth's creation that the Earth would evolve into the 5th dimension, after it had developed the reincarnation system. It is to be carried out by the plan of the Universe.

There have been numerous human races who have lived on the Earth and they were evolved enough to move to various higher level planets. However, for the first time in the history of the Earth it will evolve into a planet of the 5th dimension itself. It is a proud moment and we cosmic beings congratulate Earth for this event. Just as a butterfly casts off its cocoon and flies into the sky, the Earth is at a stage where it has passed its juvenile period and is about to evolve as a member of the Universe by forming the body of an adult.

Therefore when the Earth has evolved, the living beings on the Earth will also be evolved at the same time and will reside here as hosts of the planet. It is not that other cosmic beings from outside will dominate and colonize the Earth.

Oh, I am relieved. I imagined cosmic beings in the fifth dimension coming down to live here when the Earth attains

the 5th dimension. By the way, looking back at the present state of the people here, it is hard to think that the Earth is changing in a good direction. The Earth is dying, eco-systems and human beings are dying too. In this condition, how can the Earth and its creatures evolve into the 5th dimension?

It is so regrettable to see the current situation of the Earth. However, when anything hits the extreme point, it is designed to change; this is also true of the Earth's condition. The end is closer when the situation reaches the extreme and that indicates a great reversion will soon begin. Remember the darkest and coldest moment is just before sunrise.

Then, do you mean right now the Earth has reached the final stage of its time in the 3rd dimension?

Everything is meant to turn over when it reaches its limitation, just as winter deepens so that it is extremely cold, spring begins and it becomes warmer. Right now the Earth is in turmoil, its body and mind are deeply wounded, which also means the time has come for it to be reborn again. Like human beings, the Earth is a living being that nurtures all living creatures who are its family, minerals, microorganisms, plants and animals. All living creatures have self-healing powers, so they can heal themselves when infected by diseases. Likewise, the Earth is about to start a self-healing process to cure itself of its own diseases.

If the Earth has self-healing powers, why has it waited in pain while it gets ruined like this? Wouldn't it have been better if it had started the healing process earlier?

Everything has its own perfect timing. The mystery of the Universe is that a great life is destined to be born in great pain like a mother needs to undergo great pain to deliver a baby. Also, a butterfly must go through the pains of cutting its flesh in the course of shedding off its husk as a chrysalis, to fly into the sky. Earth cannot be reborn into the Universe until the wounds on the Earth's body and mind turn into scabs to create new body and mind and it suffers from the pains of growth.

The Gate to the New Dimension, the "Photon Belt"

Nowadays doomsday scenarios are popular. Will everybody die and then be born again as the Earth is reborn?

No, it's not like that. By enduring all the natural disasters and the painful experiences coming to the human world, you will be better equipped to live on a new Earth in a new body and mind.

How is it possible to renew our old bodies and minds? I don't think it's possible unless there's a magic spell.

That's right. If everything were to continue on as it is now, all the living creatures and the Earth itself could not create new bodies and minds. This can only be done with the Earth's shift of dimension, the so-called "universe-scale event". We can call this a magic project of the Universe that completely transforms the Earth and its creatures. This is to be accomplished as the Earth arrives at the gate to a new dimension which exists beyond the horizon of the Universe.

The gate to the new dimension?

That's right. The Earth and all of its creatures will receive the light of life which radiates from the sun of life. And they will be transformed and be born anew.

Entering the Photon Belt and Dimensional Ascension

Oh, really? The gate to the new dimension and the light of life... What on earth are they?

They are none other than the photon belt. Now the solar system is entering the photon belt that is coming from beyond the horizon. When entering the photon belt, the Earth will be exposed to the light of life and will ascend straight forward to the 5th dimension, passing through the 4th, for the first time in the history of the Earth. We can say the photon belt is the "sun of light" and the photons coming from the photon belt are the "light of life".

The photon belt? What is it exactly and how can it change the Earth and its creatures?

As the Earth is covered by an energy field, that is the magnetic field, so each constellation has a photon belt for its energy belt.

Right now the solar system, including the Earth, which revolves around the Pleiades Constellation has entered the Pleiades' Photon Belt for the first time in

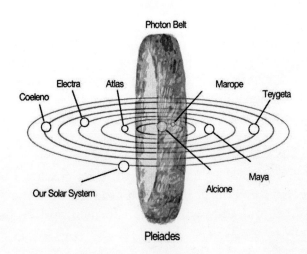

13,000 years, and is about to enter the main photon belt zone. (Refer to the picture above)

Once the Earth enters the main photon belt zone, the Earth, while receiving photons with high energy level out of the photon belt, will shift into the 5th dimension and all the creatures on the Earth as well as the Earth itself will experience a change in quality.

Will the Earth ascend to the 5th dimension?

Yes, it will. A higher dimension means the constituents of matter will change to a higher energy oscillation. If you microwave food, the state of food changes because of microwave radiation. Likewise when the Earth enters into the photon belt, atoms that constitute the Earth and all cells of creatures will be exposed to photons and will resonate with them. As the frequency of oscillation changes, the condition of matter also changes. Ultimately they will no longer be in a material state but will transform into an 'ether' condition.

Do you mean that a microwave will change only the state of the matter, whereas the photon belt would change and refresh both the body and mind?

That's right. When the dimension shifts, you will feel as if there are no external changes in the beginning. But as times passes, you will realize you have moved to another time and space or into a world of different oscillation.

Hearing what you say, I am reminded of the movie, Stargate.

That's right. You can understand when the Earth enters the center of the photon belt, it will play the role of a dimensional gate.

What are photons and the photon belt?

Everything in the Universe breathes. The photon belt is an energy field created as all creatures release their energy outwardly when they breathe. And photons are the energy particles emitted to the outside through the photon belt. Accordingly, we can say it is not that only constellations have their photon belt, but all stars, planets and even creatures have their own photon belt.

I have a new understanding of the meaning of the photon belt. You mean every living being that breathes has its own photon belt?

Yes. In the case of human beings, they form their aura fields around them through consciousness activities; we can say these are also kinds of photon belts and the aura is the photon energy of a human being.

How is the role of the photon belt related to the dimensional leap?

The purpose of the Universe is evolution, and it has moved the wheels of its history for that purpose without any break at all and has now reached this time. That the Universe evolves means that all celestial bodies and living beings which make up the Universe will develop into creatures that have a higher consciousness. The Universe revolves spirally and when the time arrives, it will transfer to higher level of evolution cycle and will develop. Although the Universe evolves linearly, when the time comes, it will make a leap in its evolution. What makes it possible is the photon belt.

I didn't know that the photon belt performs such a critical role. Then, what kind of energy is the photon that comes from the photon belt?

The photon is light energy; there're two kinds of light. One is the light that comprises the material world such as infrared rays, visible rays, ultraviolet rays and cosmic rays. The other is the spiritual energy waves that form life that is non-material and which the spiritual world is comprised of. Scalar waves, which Earth people vaguely know about but don't know how to use, fall under the spiritual energy waves.

Scalar waves? What are they?

We can say Scalar waves are the light of life that delivers life and spiritual energy; telepathy is also a sort of Scalar wave. On the other hand the spiritual energy waves, which constitute life and the spiritual world, can be transmitted at infinite speed unlike electromagnetic waves, which form material. Also, they are not influenced by gravity at all so they can pass through black holes freely. It can be called the light of "yang" since it can move freely, liberated from all restrictions.

A Magnetic Field is a Celestial Body's Photon Belt

You said all things that breathe form their own energy field and that is what photon belts are. Then what kind of photon belt do celestial bodies (planets and stars) form?

They emit magnetism in the process of breathing and emit their internally condensed thermal energy outwardly. The magnetic field formed by that process can be said to be the photon belt the celestial bodies create.

What kind of influence does the magnetic field of a celestial body have on the living beings that live there?

A magnetic field directly influences the activities of a star or planet's vitality or consciousness. A living being's sense of direction is formed by the magnetic field and their memorizing ability is made, using magnetism. Migratory birds and whales can move far away and return because of magnetic fields. But, what's more important is that the magnetic field influences the consciousness abilities of every living being.

So, the magnetic field does not just provide direction for living beings, but it influences the consciousness abilities of them, is that right?

Yes. The magnetic field does not only influence the consciousness of living beings that live on a celestial body, but it also performs the role of storing the collective consciousness of those living beings. Therefore, if the celestial bodies' magnetism changes, it can greatly affect the consciousness of every living being who lives on those celestial bodies.

In our solar system, there are 9 planets in rotation with the sun at the center. What kind of photon belt is created by our solar system?

Your sun is a star which occupies 99% of the entire mass of your solar system. The energy field created by the sun is the photon belt of your solar system. Since the sun emits energy as it breathes, it has breathing pores, which include the sun's two poles and its sunspots. The magnetic field made by them is the sun's photon belt.

The sun forms various magnetic fields according to the activities of sunspots, and affects its surroundings through solar wind. In particular, solar storms directly influence the magnetic fields of the planets in the solar system. If the sunspot activities get stronger, solar winds will break through the sun's atmosphere and will spread out into the space of the Universe, generating solar storms.

Okay. Although the scientists of the Earth don't appear to acknowledge the photon belt created by the Pleiades star cluster, since you say it exists, what is it really like?

The principle of the Universe is applied consistently from small things to bigger ones. In this sense, the Pleiades star cluster which consists of stars is also breathing and exchanging energies with external star clusters and its photon belt is the energy field that comes from the center of its star cluster. Even if the current science of the Earth cannot detect this energy, it's obvious that this energy exists in the Universe. Your solar system enters into the Pleiades star cluster's photon belt on a cycle of 13,000 years while rotating around this star cluster.

What is the characteristic of this photon belt? Does a dimensional ascension take place if our solar system enters it?

It affects your solar system, and the solar system has already entered the Pleiades star cluster's photon belt several decades ago. However, since it has not yet entered the main region of the photon belt, extreme phenomena such as a dimensional shift has not occurred yet. But, the planets of your solar system are going through many changes currently. The axis of rotation and the magnetic field of each planet have been changing a lot, and their tectonic activities are also becoming more active.

Sunspot activity has become more active, is it also related to the photon belt?

Yes. Although your sun has various cycles of sunspot activity like the ones which occur every 11 and 22 years, sunspot activity becomes more active recently than before because of the photon belt. The fact that the movement and speed of the magnetic poles gets faster and the Earth's magnetic field is rapidly decreasing, is also due to the complex influences of various photon belts affecting the earth.

What's the reason that the magnetic fields of the planets in our solar system are becoming unstable?

That is the sign which informs us that each planet has commenced its cleansing activity in preparation for its dimensional ascension. The magnetic field change means that the core energy within the planet is actively moving. It makes the tectonic activities on the planet increase, and brings about changes of living beings' consciousness.

Then, would you give us some information about the Photon Belt of the galactic system and the Universe?

The bigger the star cluster is, the higher the oscillation frequency of energy emitted from the center of the cluster is. The Pleiades star cluster emits higher vibrational energy than the solar system. The galactic system emits higher oscillation energy than the Pleiades star cluster. And the Milky Way emits higher vibrational energy than the galactic system. That's the sequence.

Are all of those photon belts periodically activated?

Yes. The bigger the group, the longer the cycle of its photon belt. Your solar system enters the photon belt of Pleiades on a 13,000-year cycle. The Pleiades star cluster enters the galactic system's photon belt on about an 110,000,000 year cycle. And the galactic system enters the Universe's photon belt on a several thousand million year cycle.

I'd like to confirm one more thing regarding the cycle of the photon belt. Is our solar system affected only by the photon belt of the Pleiades star cluster? Or is it also influenced by the photon belts of the galactic system and of the Universe?

That is such an important question. The year 2012, when the major cycle mentioned in the Mayan calendar ends, is actually a moment when several cycles of the Universe end all together.

The influence of the photon belts is getting stronger accordingly, because the Universe enters a new cycle after that time period. Your solar system is currently being affected by the influences of the photon belt of the Universe, of the galactic system, and of the Pleiades star cluster, all at the same time. And their intensity is increasing getting more and more.

Ah! I'm glad I asked about that. When will those influences of the photon belts reach their peak on the Earth?

The year 2013, will be the first year that various cycles of the Universe end and new cycles begin; and it is the year that several cycles of sunspots will also overlap. The Earth will be influenced by 4 photon belts, the sun's photon belt plus 3 photon belts = 4, not 7 photon belts.

Accordingly, the dimensional ascension process of the Earth is anticipated to begin in the period of years 2012 and 2013, after being affected by the fully-fledged influences of those photon belts. The purification activities of the Earth are anticipated to increase noticeably from the year 2011. And by the year 2025 at the latest, the Earth will have completed its dimensional leap, and will emerge as a member of the Universe and an advanced new planet.

Scientists are very concerned about solar storms and geomagnetic reversal[1]. NASA has said a solar storm, on an unprecedented scale, will occur in May, 2013. Can we anticipate the scale of damages caused by the solar storm?

2013 will be the year when the Pleiades star cluster, the galactic system, and the Universe system begin their new rhythm. Because of that, it's very likely that a more serious solar storm than ever will occur. And it will interfere in the terrestrial magnetism and cause electromagnetic storms, which will bring about huge damage on power transmission systems, and operating electric apparatus, etc. According to the state of the terrestrial magnetic field, much bigger damage can occur than the scientists of the Earth are anticipating.

How is the geomagnetic reversal related to the solar storm?

If the terrestrial magnetic field is in a normal condition, the solar storm will not damage people very much because the terrestrial magnetic field blocks cosmic rays, but it could affect electric installations and equipment. If however, the terrestrial magnetic field decreases rapidly, the situation will become different. In that case, the life of human beings on the Earth will become unsafe too, because the outer cosmic rays will pour into the Earth directly. The actual timing of the geomagnetic reversal is very critical. If the timing differs

---

[1] This happens when there is a change in the orientation of the Earth's magnetic field-the north and south magnetic positions change.

from the timing of the occurrence of the solar storm, the amount of human casualties will be small. But, if the solar storm comes at the time when the magnetic field has been reduced a lot by the geomagnetic reversal, you will meet the worst case scenario.

I am very concerned about this issue. I hope that if the solar storm has to come, that at least the magnetic field would stay intact. Can we know the exact timing of the geomagnetic reversal?

Because they're many variables involved, it's difficult to anticipate the exact timing. Since the terrestrial magnetic field is currently in a very unstable state, the situation is that the geomagnetic reversal could take place at any time. One of the reasons that the terrestrial magnetic field became unstable to the extent it is currently, is because of the excessive usage of electromagnetic waves by human beings.

Are the electro waves from cell phones relevant to climate change and natural disasters?

They are. The abuse of electro waves and the disturbance of the Earth's magnetic field caused by it are another cause that brings about abnormal climatic conditions and the Earth's purification activity.

As I have told you previously, the Earth itself is a gigantic living creature comprised of all living and non-living creatures. All living creatures breathe and take in energies they need to maintain their life. For breathing, there is a huge device to receive and release energies inside the Earth; this is the core of the Earth.

The core is not only a hollow sphere that can store the energy of emptiness but it is also an energy exchanger that can exchange the outer energy and the internal energy of the Earth. The Earth's core condenses its inner heat and transforms it into electricity and magnetism. By releasing them, the Earth cleanses itself; as a result, it radiates terrestrial magnetism. On the other hand, the Earth absorbs cosmic rays and electromagnetic waves from outer space; and it takes advantage of them as energy to improve the circulation of its own heat by refining them in itself.

The Earth is constantly exchanging signals among cells to synchronize itself to the flow of the entire body. The strength of electric signals delivered among cells is so minute, but the frequency of the signals is very similar to that of cell phones humankind uses. This is the cause of huge misery for people of the Earth. When you use cell phones, it affects the signal interchange between cells and this causes the immune system of cells in the human body to be confused; consequently that triggers various kinds of cancers.

The electromagnetic waves used by the people of the Earth keep accumulating in the space between the ionosphere and the surface of the Earth. The space is a sort of tunnel that traps electromagnetic waves. Those trapped waves are concentrated at the poles and flow into the Earth, using the Earth's magnetic field as a passage.

They are absorbed into the outer core that generates the magnetic field of the Earth. The waves affect the activities of electric currents and make the magnetic fields of the Earth unstable. Also, they provide the cause of the natural disasters such as diastrophism by influencing even the mantle.

How is the geomagnetic reversal related to the Earth's dimension leap?

The geomagnetic reversal is the last purification function the Earth will take; it will erase the collective consciousness of the Earth trapped in the Earth's magnetic field. In that process, souls in the 4th dimension, that is the Realm of Spirit of the Earth will be freed from their limitations for a while, and a new chance will be given to the advanced souls who choose to come to the Earth.

What will happen to the spirits who have deceased on the Earth? Are they going to revive and live together with us on the Earth?

Not all of them. The evolved spirits amongst those who have died can be revived on the new Earth at this time and live again, but spirits who haven't evolved enough will move to the Realm of Spirit of another planet of low dimension as the planet develops it. That is because while the Earth transfers to the 5th dimension, its Realm of Spirit in the 4th dimension will not be able to endure the high energy of the new Earth.

Then, I think we mustn't die now at this opportune time? If we die, doesn't it mean that we cannot come back to the Earth again?

It's true. When a person dies, he/she enters the Realm of Spirit in the 4th dimension. But the Earth's Realm of Spirit is scheduled to move to another planet, it will be hard for anyone to come back to the Earth again.

That the Earth enters the photon belt and its dimension ascends at this time was planned on the scale of the Universe as a part of the Grand Earth Project, from the moment the Earth was created. The project is aiming at the Universe's evolution by producing a high level of living beings through this project.

It would be wonderful if the people on the Earth could at least remember the promise they made before they came

even if they don't have other memories. If they could do so, lots of people could prepare well and could transform themselves into the New Mankind, couldn't they? I feel so sorry that many people do not know about this fact.

> There has been no more important period than now, throughout the entire history of the Earth. The words of all the Saints who have appeared up until now were to help people prepare because they knew this time was coming to the Earth. We cosmic beings truly hope many people will prepare for this better and will get on board, on the new Earth, the spaceship that will aviate to the Universe and a lot of cosmic beings who are working in and outside of the Earth and also in the Universe to help the Earth.

Cosmic beings-thank you for helping the Earth. I'd like to know about the Earth's great transformation that will appear as the Earth enters the photon belt. As you mentioned before, the process falls under the process where the Earth and its living beings cleanse their bodies and minds and move on to the new dimension, right?

Chapter 5

The Changes Caused by the Entrance into the Photon Belt

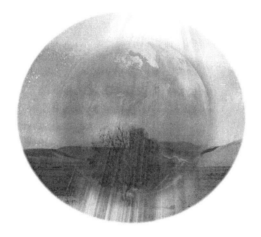

T he Earth's self-purification is its preparation for evolution into the 5th dimension. It's the process of purifying the body and mind of the Earth. We can say its body is the sky, the ground and the oceans. The mind of the Earth is the consciousness and unconsciousness that the living beings on the Earth have created collectively. And a purification process will be made for them.

What restrictions are there in the body and mind of the Earth currently?

Since the body of the Earth is made up of 3 dimensional materials, it is affected by gravity and is much restricted in its movement through time and space. The mind of the Earth is not free either. The living beings on the Earth are programmed to evolve through the reincarnation process between the material world of the 3rd dimension and the Realm of Spirit in the 4th dimension, So the collective conscious and unconscious that living beings have made meanwhile are intertwined in the course of their process of reincarnation.

Then what state is it that the Earth comes to have the body and mind of the 5th dimension, as the Earth completes its dimensional ascension?

The Earth will cleanse the dirt of its body and mind through a self-purification process and will be reborn into a more balanced body and mind. The body of the Earth which is comprised of the sky, ground, and oceans, will go through a large-scale purification process. The mind of the Earth is made up of the collective consciousness and the Ream of Spirit.

Would you explain the purification process of the sky, ground and oceans?

Currently, the sky of the Earth has been contaminated by air pollution and greenhouse gases have poured into the air such as carbon dioxide and methane, which are accelerating global warming. All the glaciers of the north and south poles will melt by 2015 because of that. And natural disasters such as floods, droughts, severe cold, intense heat, heavy snow and typhoons are taking place all over the world as the convection currents and ocean currents are changed. From 2011, extremely unusual weather phenomena will occur all over the Earth.

This makes me depressed. I think, to some extent, the unusual weather phenomena might be from man-made disasters caused by human beings, not "natural" disasters.

That is the case because the level of purification that the Earth needs depends on the degree of environmental pollution caused by human beings, and a high degree of purification process will become necessary since the environment and ecosystem of the Earth have been heavily damaged by human beings' severe egoism.

Then, how will the purification process for the ground and oceans be done?

Humans have excessively exploited energy and resources and have destroyed forests. Furthermore, they have just consumed them and have buried garbage thoughtlessly. Because of that, the ground and the oceans are dying from desertification and heavy-metal contamination. The electromagnetic waves produced by human beings have polluted the space of the Earth, and the garbage and noise pollution made by the ships in the oceans have greatly contaminated the seas.

Because of all of these things, the Earth cannot breathe and is dying. The Earth needs to create activities that help to keep its passages open for breathing. Those activities are earthquakes, tsunamis, and the eruption of volcanoes. Those are for the Earth's own survival, and the Earth has begun to intensify those activities. The 9.0 magnitude earthquake which took place in the northeastern area of Japan in March, 2011 was just the beginning. All over the Earth in 2012, much stronger earthquakes and tsunamis than that of Japan will occur and volcanoes will erupt.

You've explained about the process of how the Earth purifies its body – the sky, ground, and oceans. How is the Earth going to purify its mind, which is the actual consciousness of the Earth?

> The mind of the Earth is made up of the blending between the living beings' collective consciousness and the collective unconscious that the Realm of Spirit of the 4th dimension has. The best method to purify the mind of the Earth is for the living beings on the Earth to love each other with single-mindedness, thereby raising their levels of consciousness. If Earth people give up their egoism and return to the mind that loves nature and people then the Earth could heal the wound of its mind rapidly, and could drastically ease the degree of natural disasters to come.

Ah, what a wonderful method! But, I wonder whether the humans who get the Earth into this terrible situation because of their egoism and greed, are able to change the collective conscious of the Earth with one-mindedness. Will it be possible?

> It's never something impossible. As we can learn from the case of "the 100th monkey effect," if everyone of Earth's people put love into action, it can spread all over the world at once when the number exceed the threshold. Although it seems impossible at first that the entire humanity could achieve one-mindedness in the beginning, if people get united firmly into one entity and practice love even at one corner of the Earth, that can expand all at once and in one moment like wild fire; so we can change the collective consciousness, which is the mind of the Earth; and can relieve the level of the Earth's crisis.

What a terrific message! Even if it could be just me alone, I will start acting from love right now to save the Earth and reconstruct consciousness. Also, I need to announce this to many people to let them join.

That's right! The reason the Earth is going through its crisis now is because the efforts for small actions voluntarily made by Earth people were insufficient. If you inform many people of small actions they can share love with nature and other people and practice those actions consistently, many people will be able to pass through the Earth's great change and will survive as the New Mankind.

I understand. Thank you for your wonderful message.

Part 3

Chapter 6

The Changes the Earth will face while passing the Photon Belt

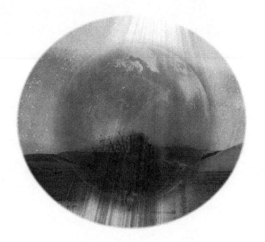

Marlin, Can I ask how long you have been watching the Earth?

Though I haven't been there permanently, I have been watching the Earth for about three thousand years.

Really? Have you been watching for so long? Why?

We have been watching the Earth for a much longer time. I mean that I have been doing the duty for about three thousand years. It takes direct and indirect participation and support of much more beings than is thought for a planet to go through an evolutionary process and shift its dimension. No planet can evolve and go through a dimension shift on its own.

74

As seniors, we have been waiting for our juniors to develop well. We have been waiting till now in order to make a contribution of our own to the evolution of the Earth. We have had less direct participation than other planets of the fifth dimension. Just a few cosmic beings of our planet went down to the Earth and did their duties.

Have you been waiting for this moment?

Yes, we have. But if the Earth didn't go through this process well now, its schedule might change. You might stay on the Earth. Otherwise, you might move to another planet. You will move along with human history. Even now, new lives are being planted and attempted on new planets. You will see them sometime.

Then, you mean that many cosmic beings were scheduled to play their own roles from the beginning in generating and evolving human beings, don't you?

That goes for other planets, too. But the Earth is different in that beings of high dimension which even we cannot know participate directly and in many cases they come down to the Earth and play some kind of role. Just from that fact, we can know that the Earth is so special. And there are high-dimensional energies on the Earth which even we haven't experienced. It is such a wonderful phenomenon because the level of most of the human beings of the Earth is too low.

Unusual Changes of Weather and Social Confusion

You said that it is expected that unusual changes of weather will cause terrible social confusion. I have been doing meditation for many years and I have been quite interested in the ways of the world. But I have some doubts about whether the destiny of the Earth, or the future of the Earth,

is really predetermined as you predicted yesterday. I know that the Earth has a characteristic that it depends much on the thoughts or the will of human beings. How do you predict that such things will happen without fail this year and next year? Is it a prophecy or something like a prospect of scientists?

It seems more correct to say that it is not a prophecy but a prospect based on the conditions which human beings and the Earth are under. A prophecy is usually made without being based on any specific causes and effects or phenomena. If you are told that something would happen at some time after a couple of years but you don't know the related causes and effects such as why it would happen, then it is a prophecy.

Yet, what I am telling you now is not a prophecy. This is a prediction. Based on the karma of human beings as results and activities of what they have done till now, I predict what will happen in the future. If you collect plenty of information and analyze it, you could predict the future in full. Humans on the Earth can make such predictions too, but your predictions are very limited with present human technology and ability to collect information.

We cosmic beings possess a lot more advanced scientific technology and we have been watching the Earth precisely for many years. Thus, we can predict the situation of the Earth much better than you can. As the Earth itself has many variables, it is difficult to predict exact times in units of days or hour. But we can predict almost exactly the general flow of this year and the next, and furthermore, the general flow of a year.

Scientists of the Earth have been concerned about the unusual changes of weather and made predictions about them. But it is difficult for them to predict exactly when they

will happen and different scientists make different predictions. That's a problem.

I am not ignoring humans of the Earth, but human beings know less than 1% of all the information about their own planet, the Earth. How many of the present theories on the Earth are well-grounded and recognized? How is the Earth formed? How many living creatures live on the Earth? For what was the planet Earth created? They don't know anything correctly.

You're right. Once I studied the problems of nature and ecological systems. At that time I felt keenly that people don't know anything. People just guess about trivial natural phenomena, or about relations between animals and plants. There were very few things about them which were explained.

That's right. But that's not because you were a non-professional in that field. So-called professionals on the Earth are not different essentially. They just know better than ordinary people that they don't know anything.

I think that you are right. "People of the Earth don't know anything…" Then how much do cosmic beings know about the Earth? You say that you have much advanced technology. How advanced is your technology? You may be too proud of yours.

Every planet is different. Advanced planets can be said to be scores of thousands of years more advanced than the Earth. But such a comparison does not have great meaning. The principle of the Universe is that one can get an upgrade by being awakened in a moment while one may stay at one place by repeating one's lives.

The biggest problem of the technology of the Earth is that it is confined within the material world.

There is hardly anything in the Universe that can be done with the technology which human beings have based on material. To put it plainly, the technology is a knowledge which is only useful within one's village. Even though a leader might be proud that he has much knowledge compared to others kids in a village, what could he show off at Oxford or Harvard University?

Hmm, you hurt our pride a little, but I think you are right.

The material-centered technology of human beings cannot go beyond the solar system. However, we cosmic beings can come to the Earth from our planets which are thousands of light years away and talk to you as we do now. We look at the world and at the Universe from fundamentally different viewpoints. When you get over the limitations of your imagination, you human beings will be able to take part in the Universe as citizens of the Universe.

I think I understand what you are saying, but I still have many questions. You said that we will have extremely unusual changes of weather this year and next year. I think they will probably have great ripple effects on the whole of society. Obviously, a food crisis can be expected. Would you please explain how they will have an effect on the whole of society?

The food crisis caused by unusual changes of weather has already begun. As I mentioned before, because the crops were in bad condition last year in the Northern Hemisphere and this winter in the Southern Hemisphere, food prices have already risen a lot. When the harvest figures of the Southern Hemisphere are specifically known, the food prices will soar higher. Furthermore, as the major international grain suppliers understand this situation and control the supply and demand of grains, the food price is highly likely to rise up even more sharply.

To what level will the food prices rise this year?

In the latter half of 2011, the food prices will go up three to five times higher than before.

Three to five times? If the prices rise so high, I think world-wide riots will start probably this year. I am not sure of the numbers, but I remember reading a newspaper article that food crises of 2007 and 2008 caused great food disturbance and riots in about 40 countries.

Of course this is only the average price rise. Food prices will go up less than those numerical values in developed countries, yet this will be different in each country. Depending on how many breadbaskets you have in your country, how much food you can supply locally, and how much food your country has stored, bigger variables may occur. However, most countries have not preserved a lot of food. Thus, most of them won't have enough food to sustain themselves during the crisis.

Developing and underdeveloped countries will suffer much bigger effects, won't they?

Yes, they will. Countries with some national strength or resources would be able to solve the problems diplomatically, but other countries would be the very targets of the disturbance.

I can anticipate great turmoil.

That's right. The food crisis is the very matter of survival. That is not only the problem of individual survival but also of national survival. Riots will emerge immediately in the countries where public peace and order is not fully maintained or where the level of national consciousness is low. Local wars are highly likely to happen within countries. Of course, the external causes of the wars will not be food issues. Though wars may happen for other reasons, problems of survival such as food and water will be behind them.

You said that we will have more unusual changes of weather and a bigger food crisis in 2012. What will their impact be?

The chaos will reach its peak in 2012. The Earth is one organism. If one region suffers from starvation and this causes conflicts between different regions, similar events will flare up in many different regions all at once and that will turn into a global issue. The food crisis is not something that even developed countries can avoid but at the same time, the food crisis in developing countries will expand globally as well. This is the meaning of the so called "global village." That is because people of the entire Earth are actually groups who are sharing a common destiny.

Would you please tell us more specifically about the crisis?

The crisis due to climate change is not simply limited to the food supply only. By 2012, the economic system of most countries in the world will nearly be paralyzed. When the food supply is not enough, the prices of commodities will jump and people will suffer from the grim realities of life. Enterprises will collapse. Governments will try to quickly extinguish the flames but there are hardly any governments that can cope with emergent situations that occur all at once. These are events which are unheard of.

A decisive factor in this will be the energy crisis. The current Earth civilization is too dependent on oil. The oil production has already hit the peak. It means you have already passed Peak Oil a while ago. On the top of that, natural disasters due to climate change in 2011 and 2012 will be fatal to major oil producing countries. The demand for oil will become higher while the oil supply will decrease dramatically. This will cause serious disturbances to transport and key industries.

That makes me sigh once again. After calming myself down, I will ask specific questions. You've said the climate change will influence the world's oil supply. Will earthquakes strike major oil-producing countries? Or will it affect them in other, different ways?

There won't be many countries that will be free from earthquakes in 2012. Earthquakes will simultaneously take place on a global basis. Most countries in the circum-Pacific belt will be fatally affected, yet the Earth has begun its activity to purify the whole Earth, so earthquakes won't be only be the problem of the countries around the circum-Pacific belt.

Of course it is not that all major oil producing countries will stop supplying oil due to earthquakes. It is more correct to say that oil processing system and its delivery system are to be paralyzed, rather than that the land containing the oil itself will be buried. Even if there is oil, it will become difficult to pump it up and distribute it to the country which needs it. Even oil delivery by sea will be so unstable due to frequent disruptive weather events, that it will be impossible to meet the needs of the market on time. For many reasons that make the supply unstable, the oil price will go up dramatically.

I remember when the whole world went into crisis because the oil price rose up to 100 dollars per barrel.

Countries such as the US, will try hard to hold the oil price back. By the beginning of 2012, the oil price will rise twice or three times higher than now but at some point it will get out of control and it will rise dramatically to an extent you cannot imagine.

Unimaginable price?

As the oil price soars, food prices will rise sharply as well, being interlocked with the oil issue. It is because a factor that increases food price as well as oil price will be reflected at the same time. Thus, the food price in 2012 will also become beyond your imagination. The problem is not the money. Even if you have money, you won't be able to purchase food. At the time when the harvesting season of the Northern Hemisphere passes by, the voices filled with tremendous pain will cover the Earth.

I suddenly feel depressed. Do you mean there will be starvation all over the world? Is it possible for such situations to happen in our present civilization?

Of course, you will not be able to imagine that happening. The imagination of human beings is originally limited and people naturally want to turn their faces away from those facts. However, looking a little more calmly into the situation, you will find that it is not just a rhetorical expression threatening the people on the Earth. People have already gone too far. Many countries just conceal the facts about their food, oil, and so on for their interests. If you examine just the rough flow, you will find that they have been running without any brakes. They have run without any brakes and they already stand on the edge of a precipice.

If people cannot purchase food, many complicated social problems will probably occur.

Yes. Riots and plundering will be the norm all the time, and governments will not be able to maintain public peace. It is also obvious that many people will suffer from depression or commit suicide. To make matters worse, illness and contagious diseases will be prevalent, however the governments won't be able to cope with them because they lack the capability and resources to tackle such circumstances.

In one word, the state will be anomic. Yet, how things will proceed might look different in each country and each region. Some countries and regions will make efforts to share such sufferings and correct their problems little by little. Other countries and regions will not manage to escape their situations of disorder and plundering, and will be on the way to collapse together.

I see. I would like to stop here and ask more specific questions about the aspects of the crisis.

All right. I will tell you as specifically as possible. That is the way to reduce the coming crisis even a little. We try to converse with you human beings and visit the Earth because we have intentions of warning you of such a future and reduce the crisis by making you look back at yourselves even now, because the Earth and our planet are connected to each other and are one group sharing a common destiny. Many cosmic beings have been watching and loving the Earth. Although some negative interventions of cosmic beings have caused many side effects on the Earth, many good cosmic beings think that the Earth must not be left alone any longer than it has been.

I understand. I would like to know what the major patterns of the crisis which will be caused by abnormal weather phenomena will be. Shall we begin from earthquake and tsunami, or with droughts and floods?

Earthquakes will be the major aspect of the crisis to surface externally. An earthquake itself has a great ripple effect. It makes buildings collapse, it destroys roads and causes many casualties. After the earthquake, it brings about numerous suffererings. The tsunamis which follow earthquakes destroy coastal areas completely and cause many casualties and the destruction of facilities. Because the earthquake is a visible disaster, it will definitely cause humans' panic and chaos. Especially this year (2011) and next year (2012), unprecedented gigantic earthquakes will occur, and people will suffer to the extreme from the direct damage and the psychological chaos which will result from them.

Is it possible to predict when and where the earthquake will take place and with what magnitude?

All of the countries located in the circum-Pacific orogenic zone, including Japan will be damaged by the earthquakes. It will be unprecedented. The island countries such as the Philippines and Indonesia will be greatly damaged and Australia will not be an exception. Especially, the USA will be damaged greatly because of their karma they've incurred meanwhile.

The timing will differ depending on the regions. Even if earthquakes have already occurred frequently in many regions, a gigantic earthquake of more than magnitude 8.0 will begin in the second half of this year, and they will frequently hit all areas next year.

Then, substantial areas of the Earth will have gone through the great chaos visibly, before entering the main photon belt zone, won't they?

Yes. You must understand that the great chaos will have already begun from the end of this year, or next year. Although the timing to pass through the photon belt has been determined as being after next year, the great chaos of the Earth will start before that.

I feel strange listening to natural disasters so specifically like this.

Actually it will not be that serious if it's just one crisis of unusual weather phenomena or a food crisis or an energy crisis. But what makes matters serious is that they will come in a bunch simultaneously from the second half of this year and next year and will cause various social problems and chaos. It's been said there's no time because of that. You must get ready for everything before that, and let people know this situation so that they can get some understanding and prepare for this situation.

I see. I return to the subject again. How about circulation of water? I mean drought or flood. It also includes typhoons.

Earth has already fallen in the structure where its water cannot circulate normally. Likening the Earth to human body, its circulatory disease has been so severe that its air and nutrition have not circulated normally. Because of that, various organic diseases and cancers have occurred here and there. If you had that body, what would it be?

I think it would be hard to survive for several months.

Right. The Earth is not very different. Severe drought and flood have already brought about huge damage and pain, earthquakes are also showing different movement compared to last year. It's the pain of Mother Earth that is not endurable any more, and it's making an effort to heal it.

I understand. Are all of these unusual weather phenomena caused by global warming? Some scholars claim that they're not because of global warming but because of cosmic rays which affect cloud layers and produce ions in the atmosphere. The cosmic rays here refer to particle and radioactivity that are pouring into Earth from the Universe. The

scholars who claim this also acknowledge that human activity affects climate change, but they say that human activity is just a secondary factor and that the major factor is cosmic rays. What do you think about this?

It's right that current abnormal weather phenomena have been caused by global warming for the most part. The Earth has been heated but it could not handle the heat and has tried to refine it or emit it. Such efforts have been revealed as the purification process of the Earth. In a human body also, if its balance is broken, it finds its balance again by releasing the heat. Similarly, the Earth also responds through various activities in order to fundamentally solve the inner heat and the rise in temperature caused by that.

Your words paint a vivid picture and make me feel scared.

You may imagine the movie, "2012". It will be real. But don't be so sad. Viewing from the outlook of the Universe, it'll be a new birth for the Earth. The earth will wear new energy clothes and will change its dimension. Those who will survive will get a new foundation and chance.

May I hear more about the conditions at the end of 2012. A book says Earth will pass through a tunnel and will be moved near Sirius, the day and the night will last 24 hours each for some time, and it'll take a week to pass the null zone that is, the entrance of photon belt. Is it right?

You may think that 70% of the books written by channellers on the market are the messages from ETs mixed with their intention. It seems that they deliver many good words, but they include their own intention. The intention means they want to foster many earthlings to follow them. The content of the book you've mentioned is the same partially. The cosmic being that sent the message to the channeller also doesn't know the whole picture.

It could never happen that Earth deviates out of its determined orbit and moves to another zone by the will of cosmic beings. Actually, the fate of the earth is an affair that whoever the being is in the Universe, they cannot dare to speak of it. No matter how advanced the cosmic being is, they don't have such capability and authority that they could determine the fate of Earth.

At one time, the beings from the planets that were in an early stage of migrating to the 5th dimension where good and evil coexisted, came to Earth, interfered with it and made numerous conflicts. But now it will not be allowed any more. In other words, your solar system will inevitably follow a pre-determined orbit. And Earth will follow the same path as a planet after an escalation in its dimension, as if it follows the course of evolution which rises spirally up the same zone.

If humankind on the Earth attain great dimensional ascension and achieve their evolution, maybe they will move to a new planet and Earth might start its new history as an educational planet after the seeds of humans have been sown again from the beginning. Actually, we also don't know this portion of information exactly.

However, during the process, the axis of the Earth is straightened, you will experience the absence of light and there will be a position shift, as if the ground and the sky would be shifted towards each other. It might be 1 or 2 weeks at the end of 2012 that the earth and the sky will fluctuate as if you are afloat in the air. Actually, viewing from the perspective of the

Universe, this moment will be the same as the time when a baby is born and first cries out. Pain follows of course. But, those who are qualified will share the pain and be reborn together with the Earth.

As I've listened to you, I think we're going to face a miserable reality even if we remain alive.

Right, because the purification process will also be done to human beings. Many people will lose their lives due to no drinking water, food and diseases, before the photon belt arrives.

The influence of the photon belt is the destruction of immunity, to explain it easily. It will change the electron structure of cells of the human body and turn off its immune system instantly. It's not easy to survive at the site of disasters with a feeble immune system. Photon energy is spiritual energy. Thus, the change of immune system will be influenced by the entity's degree of spiritual purity. This strong beam will divide life and death by that standard.

How will it be after 2013?

You will go through intense cold like an ice age over half of the year 2013. Grass and trees will not be able to grow yet and the sky will continue to be gray. Depending on regions, volcanoes will erupt or earthquakes will occur sporadically. China will experience a continuous tectonic shift even in this period. The current geographical features of China will be changed entirely, and they'll find that the sea becomes land, and the land becomes the sea.

In 2014, light will begin to enter the sky little by little, and the temperature will gradually rise. But it'll not be ready for plants to grow yet. Those who survive until that time will be the chosen ones, and you may see them as the ones who've adapted to the photon belt. The sea level which will have risen suddenly, will go down gradually, and the coast line will begin to stabilize. Those who survive will build communities locally for their further survival. They'll utilize remaining resources and come up with measures to survive. Traffic and communication will be destroyed and will have not been restored yet.

Exchange will begin little by little in 2015. People will be able to use transport and communication partially. It'll be possible to use an infinite power supply system by this time.

You've said that vegetables can't grow for some time, then unless we store food in advance, there's no possibility to survive even if we don't die by chance, is there?

Mankind survived even in the ice age. There are always groups that adapt to the environment. There'll be animals and plants who will survive together with human beings, and they will become the new ancestors of Earth. Also, you'll feel your appetite and dietary life change to a natural one.

Chapter 7

The Conditions Before and After the Entry into the Photon Belt

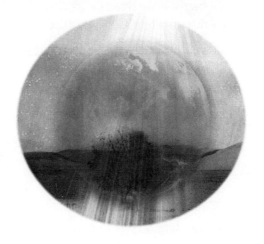

We've explored our subject by year. I think that there is a photon belt at the center of all of these changes. So, I want to know about natural phenomena before passing the photon belt and the damages which are caused by that.

The photon belt means energy, and before huge energy comes, some signs are always given. The current climate change can also be said to be a kind of sign.

Because an energy storm that is huger than a tsunami has already entered your solar system, each realm (system) is preparing a response to that. Since a head-to-head contest could mean an explosion, they are disarming themselves in order to accept the energy and let it pass through them.

Nature has been causing numerous changes. It's only human beings who have not been ready. It's because the society that humans have made, has caused the side effect of distancing people from nature.

If you observe the current changes of nature, many of you can find very unusual, first-ever weather patterns that you've never seen before. The Earth is facing huge change for the first time, so "First-ever" is an appropriate word to describe it.

The current struggle for change is to restore the beauty of the Earth and to prepare for the shift into the new era.

You have mostly explained about how human beings' damage has caused natural disasters; but how about the damage of nature itself? The damage that the animals and plants of nature will suffer from also concerns me because they've been sharing all the joys and sorrows with humans.

Your horizon is becoming wider. It's a good question because you could have slanted it toward a human-centered way.

These activities being done by nature are endeavors to make the Earth a better place to live in. Those activities will result in more damages to nature itself, rather than to human beings.

Nature will be damaged greatly by landslides or the collapse of a bank after heavy rain in summer, where the forests have been destroyed by reckless logging or development has been done without consideration for the environment. Especially, the majority of plants which have been artificially mutated by humans will become extinct. Instead local plants called weeds, which have lived for so long in the region, will survive.

And many of the fish which live in water will also go through many hardships because of the ongoing rain and they will suffer substantial extinction. As various substances which have been produced by humans will flow into the rivers and into the sea eventually, the ecosystem of the sea will be destroyed by heavy contamination.

There are two biological worlds coexisting on Earth, one is the world which prospers in the sun and the other is the one which prospers in the shade. In peaceful ages, the creatures which live in the sun prosper and give much help to people. But in chaotic ages, the creatures which live in the shade thrive and can make people nearly reach extinction.

Especially, numerous contagious diseases will be rampant, because the continuous heavy rains and monsoons will increase the reproduction of bacteria and fungi. Sunlight has prevented this from occurring, but because its effect will be weakened, they will prevail more. Since this will influence not only humans but animals, many of the animals will lose their life just like they died because of the foot and mouth disease last winter or the avian influenza (bird flu) in Korea.

Is that so? You have told me mainly about the rain with regard to the change of weather before the photon belt passes, but it seems to me that the chill of winter will also be formidable.

There is a considerable chance that the passing time of the photon belt which has been predicted, will be in winter. At present the temperature of Korea in winter has dropped considerably, but when the time comes, it will just be the norm that the temperature of the whole area including the most southern island of Korea, Jeju island goes below-10°C. It is likely to be much colder weather than that of last winter you already experienced. -20°C or under it may continue for a considerable period even in the southern areas. Until now -20°C in Korea was the temperature you could experience only in the central areas or mountainous districts, but as the entire region including the southern areas may be frozen due to the severe cold, a lot of damage is anticipated.

As you said, when the severe coldness comes to the south, the damage will probably be much more serious because there are too many houses that were built without the concept of insulation. Especially it is likely that there will be a serious portable water problem due to the freezing and bursting of water pipes.

The areas that were cold from old times won't have any big problems even though the temperature goes down a little bit more, but other areas will have much bigger damage.

Also it is likely to snow a lot with the cold. The snowfall of 30 to 40cm will be normal and it is quite probable that there will be many places where they have a snowfall above 1M. There will be many isolated areas in the countryside and people in cities will have transport chaos, and another problem of heavy snow is that it may cut off the supply of electricity.

Now the whole world is structured where everything would be isolated and come to a standstill without the supply of electricity. In such situation if the severe cold comes in midwinter, and the supply of electricity and water is stopped, the sensation of fear will be maximized.

Even though we know about this information, it seems to me that it will actually be hard to prepare for it actually.

You are right. Even though people know about the information, there won't actually be many people to prepare for it even if they believe it is true. However, even so, there is hope, because people who will prepare for it will appear. Even though only a few people prepare for that, they will be able to give a lot of help to neighboring people.

What kinds of natural phenomena will show up while we pass the photon belt?

It seems that a solar wind will cause the breakdown of numerous electronic products when they pass the photon belt. Even though the influence of the solar wind is still blocked from the atmosphere of the Earth, as the atmosphere gradually disappears, the solar wind will rage to all areas of the earth. It seems that satellites which many countries have will get damaged to a certain extent, and there is a strong chance that large-scale blackouts will occur due to the solar wind.

In order to protect machines and electronic devices, you will have to unplug them to avoid the direct influence of the solar wind. And vehicles too need to be placed inside a parking building with batteries separated. Otherwise, it is highly probable that their electronic circuits will be destroyed because they can't overcome the overcharged electrical load due to the influence of the solar wind and the photon belt. The solar wind will reach the extreme right before the Earth passes out of the photon belt, and it will gradually disappear after the pass of the photon belt.

It seems that the air pollution due to the volcanic eruptions will make half of the Korean Peninsula fill with dark clouds. Especially the areas around Mt. Baekdu are likely to be severe, and the central areas with Cheolwon being centered are anticipated to experience considerable damage. Even though the volcanic ashes will block the electromagnetic waves, etc. coming from the solar wind to a certain degree, these places are likely to have severe pollution due to the volcanic ashes. Fortunately it seems that the nuclear power plants of the Korean Peninsula will be safe yet. But I can't say for sure.

These phenomena will gradually calm down as the Earth passes the photon belt, but air pollution will continue for a considerable period due to the volcanic eruptions and fire which take place in the whole earth. As the Korean Peninsula is located at the point where the sea and the continent meet, it is quite probable that its pollutants will be more quickly eliminated than those of other places. An especially clear sky will be seen from the southern areas.

Temperatures of -30 to -40°C will continue for a considerable time due to the darkness which will last for some period. Everything will have to hibernate in the darkness. People who survive at this time will gradually be able to live a new life.

What things can people prepare for this period? It seems that they need to prepare things in advance to protect themselves from the solar wind and the cold weather.

First of all they need to prepare enough food. And they need clothes and houses to protect their bodies and to keep warm. Houses should be able to resist the earthquakes to a certain extent.

You are better off choosing a place away from the cities as far as possible, and a place with hard ground will be better. Upper areas which are far away from the seashore and the river will be a comparatively safer place. And a house which has less dangerous structure will be better, even though it may be destroyed. Houses made using panels will be easily rebuilt and will get less damage.

Do you have any other additional items that you would like to tell me about?

When the time comes, it will be almost impossible to travel. You might live in a region as wide as a town at most for several years. If you are lucky, you can interchange with each other at a county level, but if you want to go to a broader area, you will have to take a big risk.

Even now you should prepare so that you can grow your physical strength and enhance your level of immunity. However good an environment you make, you will consume your physical strength tremendously in the extreme change of weather, so it is the time that health is important. You should take care of your health in order to overcome your diseases quickly, and you had better acquire simple health care methods to take care of the health of yourself and your family. When this era comes, nobody can do it for you, so you should be able to do everything yourself.

Everything should be taken care of by oneself... It reminds me of a survival game.

You will be in the situation where it is tens of times harder to survive than a survival game. Even though the weather will become better as the Earth passes through the photon belt, it will take several years to recover. We can say that those who can take care of their lives are the prepared ones.

It looks like earthquakes, volcanic eruptions, and heavy snow will continue for 2 to 3 years, and all disasters that human beings have imagined will be integrated and will come in more severe forms. They are not happenings in imagination like you can see in the movies but are the reality that will visit you soon. It is shown through the earthquakes that hit Japan that imagination doesn't exist anymore but it is a real situation.

Only those who encounter various messages we cosmic beings deliver and take action on them will be able to overcome the difficult period. The fact that the damages to city dwellers who prefer modern civilization are more serious, is because they live without using their body much. People who have lived together with nature experiencing it directly through their body, will be able to find the method to overcome the difficult period easily. But the people who have solved everything with material means, will meet the age when they will won't be able to survive.

All of these crises are only a part of the purification process to make a beautiful new world. If they don't understand things from the standpoint of the Universe with the perspective of the Universe, they will come to destroy themselves in despair and end their lives.

I feel very sorry and concerned to hear that so many people will go through difficulties because of natural disaster, climate changes and economic crisis. What frame of mind should we have to get ourselves ready for the future?

No matter how difficult an environment it may be, humans are capable of adapting themselves to it.

Those humans, animals and plants that will survive will sprout the bud of hope so that the sick Earth can come back to new life.

Furthermore the Earth, worn out by material civilization will be purified into a beautiful planet where nature and all living beings will live in harmony. That is returning to a truly humane life. With the unique mental power and the power of optimism, people will be able to get over the great revolution. We will support you.

The Earth Is a Creature That Is Alive and Breathes

As I converse with you, I am afraid that the time of crisis is not far away. I feel humans have affected the Earth very much up until now.

Yes, that is correct. A living creature has the five viscera and the six entails. Just as each organ plays its role and creates a balance in the whole, the Earth is also a living creature and each continent makes a balance with the other continents. From the Earth's view point, each continent acts like an organ and has a relationship with each another. Thus, when you harm the land and develop it on your own, this is the same as having the organs of the Earth under your thumb and manipulating them as you like.

I will explain each continent comparing it to each organ in a living creature. Asia corresponds to the spleen and the stomach. It falls under the center of the Earth and so its role is controlling things in the center. Also it has the most population in the world, absorbs diverse cultures and digests them into their own. It means Asia has a great digestive power. It controls the whole in the middle, keeps the balance and plays a major role.

Next comes Europe. Europe is the liver and the gallbladder. Europe has explored many countries around the world and colonized them with their strong force of arms. They are also very aggressive. Such characteristics indicate that Europe is like the liver that is in charge of the whole body and kills germs. Thus the liver is called an organ of generation in oriental medicine. Its role was to take the initiative in history, but now its function has become very dull. The characteristics of Europe are to take the initiative as well as to act lively.

Then it is Africa. Africa is the kidneys and the bladder. We can know this from their dark skin and also from their excellent athlete's ability and physical strength. Africans are quite physically developed in the body. It is related to the characteristics of Africa which are applied to the Water element from amongst the Five Elements. As it is said that the origin of the current humankind is an ape from Africa, the role of Africa is Water energy, the origin of life. This is the reason why there a number of wild animals even now.

Another function of Africa is excretion. The reason that Africa became such a devastated and hot land is because its role is to excrete. Africa brings the heated energy and pollutants of the globe to its land and embraces them. It is for this reason that poverty and starvation started from their land first. Africa is holding the pain of the entire Earth now. If you do not take care of them, you should realize that you will soon suffer from the same starvation and poverty.

North America is the lungs and the large intestine. They now hold the control of the energy of the entire world. Like the lungs take charge of the energy in one's body, North America has taken the lead in terms of money and the materials of the world. It also creates money and materials and supplies them everywhere in the world. This is the role of lungs. Lungs are situated above other body organs and their role is to dominate all the other organs, to teach and to protect. They are the things North America is doing now.

South America is the simpo (pericardium) and samcho (triple warmer). As we can know from the fact that the Amazon purifies the air, South America corresponds to the simpo and samcho, it makes the earth breathe and supply fresh energy to the earth. If you destroy the rainforests of the Amazon and disturb South America from playing its role, it is like putting an end to the Earth's life. Simpo and samcho are hot and they are in charge of emotions, South Americans are very passionate and joyous. It is because of the energy of South America.

Next is Oceania. Oceania is the heart as well as the small intestine. Since Oceania is far away from a continent, it does not seem so important. However, Oceania is in the middle of all the oceans and it gives command of all the oceans. 70% of the Earth is sea. The continent that controls all those oceans is Oceania which is applied to the Fire element. Thus it so hugely affects currents of the oceans as to manage the current of the ocean like the heart which pumps out blood to the whole body. Also just like the small intestine digests food, Oceania has excellent natural assets as well as resources.

When we view the Earth as a living creature that breathes, what is the health condition of the Earth now?

We can say a person is in good health when his/her five viscera and 6 entrails help one another in a balanced way, and so it is with the Earth. The imbalance of the earth increases and its health deteriorates because humans exploit the Earth. When humans did not exploit the land as often as today, each continent would have its own characteristics and would achieve balance with all the others while having normal vital activity. They can no longer do that. Thus, humans must leave the earth as it is and seek a way to co-exist.

Chapter 8

The Forecast for the Crisis of Each Continent

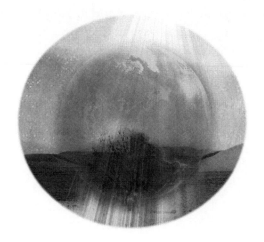

The Crisis of Oceania

Oceania is the word that generally refers to several islands around the southern Pacific. It signifies most of the pacific islands, inducing Australia, New Zealand, Melanesia and Micronesia. Its sea zone is up to 70,000,000km²; more than 10,000km² big and small islands are scattered around the area. Most of the islands fall under a tropical climate. The biggest island, Australia has the population of 20,600,000 and most of the population is concentrated along the coastal regions.

Cities in Oceania in 2011 and 2012 will be damaged by tsunami, cyclone and earthquake. Various disasters are also expected. It will take dozens or hundreds of years to purify the ocean that has been thoroughly polluted.

Would you talk about the natural disasters in Oceania? What kind of natural disasters could take place?

Cities in Oceania in 2011 and 2012 will be damaged by tsunamis. It is expected that coastal cities in Australia where buildings stand closely together and where there are many vacation areas will be damaged. The intensity of tsunamis caused by the movement of the volcanic zone in the Pacific Ocean will become more powerful every year.

The destructive power of a tsunami is something beyond people's imagination. It can crush a battleship like a piece of paper. I tell you that skyscrapers and shops around Surfers Paradise on the Gold Coast could be submerged under water.

It is possible that all the coastal cities in the Pacific Ocean can be hit by tsunamis. In the case of Australia, most cities are located on the coast, so it will be difficult for them to avoid tsunamis. It is so serious that few will expect what might happen to the beautiful Harbor

Bridge and the Sydney Opera House. It is only human beings, who are loaded with material things who will not be aware of the fact. Islands in the Pacific Ocean will be damaged by quakes and tsunamis in earnest from now on. Mother Nature will treat the Australian continent more severely.

Australia has experienced many disasters in 2010 already. Is there a particular reason why such disasters keep going on in Australia?

First is the geographical factor; Australia is facing the Pacific Ocean. Secondly, the sorrows of those who were treated unfairly in this continent have permeated into the land. In order to meet the new world, the change of the Earth is going to begin from the Pacific Ocean. Thus, we can see that it is pre-scheduled that Australia, the biggest land in Oceania will be severely damaged.

Yes, I understand. Would you tell me more specifically about disasters that will occur in Oceania in 2012?

It is expected that earthquakes will hit Oceania seriously in 2012. The circum-Pacific belt will wake up from its sleep and will create earthquakes that cannot be compared to the earthquakes of magnitude 7, which hit New Zealand last year. They will make the gem-like islands in the Pacific Ocean disappear or new islands could even arise due to volcanic eruptions.

The Crisis of Asia

As the largest continent in the world, Asia covers the middle and the east parts of the Eurasian continent. Its size is 439,700,006,000 km² (excluding the islands) and covers 30% of the land of the world, and accounts for 70% of the world population. It has an uneven population distribution; its

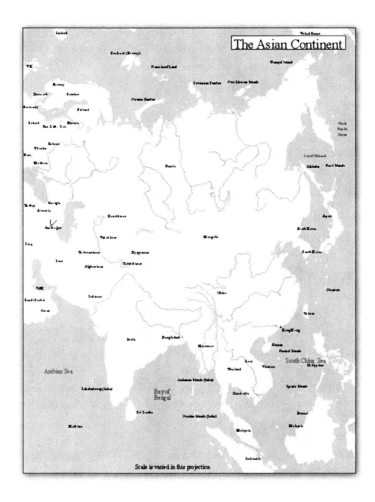

population density is the highest in the world. Its natural environment encompasses all variations, from tropical regions to cold regions, and coastal regions to dry desert regions. It has a wide variety of topography and climate.

Asia will play a role as kindling for the world's natural disasters. Many cities located along the coastlines in Southeast Asia and South Asia are within the area of influence of the earthquake belt. It is expected that earthquakes and tsunamis will strike the whole of Asia and will cause chaos.

It feels like continuous earthquakes and volcanic explosions will take place in the Circum-Pacific Belt and they will bring about a greater change in the future. Which regions will suffer a lot of damage?

All those cities located along the coastlines in Southeast Asia and South Asia will be damaged by tsunamis caused by earthquakes. Particularly, so many islands in the Pacific Ocean like in Indonesia and the Philippines are in a more dangerous situation.

It is expected that this region will play the role of a fire lighter in the world. The region can have a great influence over the geographical changes of not only Asia but also the entire Earth. Many islands in Indonesia, Japan, the Philippines and so on in the Pacific area and many cities along the coast lines in Southeast Asia and South Asia are within the scope of influence of the earthquake belt. The movement of the outer core of the Earth has begun on a full scale and therefore huge energy has begun to erupt toward the surface of the Earth.

Do you mean that the circum-Pacific belt is the starting point of global natural disasters?

Yes. It will play the role of the kindling of global natural disasters. You must have seen the power of the Indonesian tsunami. Waves as huge as the mountains struck peaceful villages and took the lives of 240,000 people in an instant.

It is expected that earthquakes and tsunamis with tens of times greater power than that will happen and will put the Asian region into chaos. Facing the power of nature, they will realize how vulnerable humans and man-built structures are.

What region will go through the biggest change due to natural disaster?

It is Northeast Asia. China, Japan and the Korean Peninsula are a vigorous region in terms of energy; they have accomplished a brilliant economic development within a short time period. There is still heavy military confrontation and hypertension in the region, but this area is important as the ending point of civilization and the starting point of a new one. It will serve as the teaching material for people of the globe, and experience extreme pains and will walk on the crossroads of life and death.

Of all Asian regions, South Asia seems most vulnerable to disasters. The region has been afflicted with drought and annual flooding. It's a pity.

As you said, Southeast Asia will be the sensitive area to climate change.

My heart is broken when I think of the people living in South Asia.

But they have cultivated an ability to maintain their lives and survive in barren land, so they will be able to display strong power at the time of crisis. Their minds are pure and they have a reverence for nature, so they will suffer less social chaos.

China in an Extremely Precarious State

I heard that they recently had snow a couple of times in Shandong Province in winter, but that other regions seem to suffer from severe drought. In many regions they haven't had even one drop of rain for several months. What is the cause of this phenomenon?

That is because of the arrogance of people who think that they can go against the will of nature. People can learn how precious something is only after they lose it. It will never be easy to prevent the upcoming abnormal climate changes from happening, even with all human wisdom and capability. China has a high likelihood of being seized by chaos with the impending disasters of heavy snowfalls, droughts, earthquakes, landslides and other hardships caused by volcanic activities, all in various areas at the same time.

What is the prospect of China's natural disasters and abnormal climate changes in 2011 and 2012?

In 2011, the signs of disaster have already begun. In 2010 unexpected damage was incurred because of the surprisingly heavy snow in the southern region. Looking at the consequences, the drought in the northern region is rising to its climax. Rainfall dropped to such a low level that it cannot be compared to previous records. For the time being, drought will continue, and that will result in considerable damage to crops. The drought and water shortage in Shandong, Henan, Hebey and around Beijing are expected to become the first wave of natural disasters and abnormal climate changes in 2011.

From 2011 the intensity and frequency will progress in a different manner from the past. The active crustal movements of China have already been proven over the last few years. The crust is known to be moving from west to east in China where the Himalayas are located. The earthquakes in Sichuan and Yushu occurred due to the collision and friction between the mantles of the crust. Because the movement of the crust and mantles have such a vast area of influence, it is difficult to accurately predict in what form its influence will manifest itself and how far it will go. The bigger problem is that preparation for it is also very limited. A real movement of earthquakes, tidal waves, and volcanic activities will begin in full scale from 2012. Natural disasters in that period will be in such a large scale that humans will be at a loss as how to handle them.

Japan: Extreme Natural Disaster in the Years 2011˜2012

Japan has been experiencing typhoons, earthquakes and even volcanoes, that is, all the biggest disasters on the Earth. Even worse, very harshly! I feel so sorry about that. Besides geographical factors, is there any other reason for that?

In many cases, natural disaster occurs as self-purification to wash off turbid energy. Through natural disaster like earthquakes and typhoons it aims to wash down polluted environment or energy. We can know natural disaster is not always negative in that aspect. Likewise you should see the change of the Earth happening currently as a process where Mother Nature cleanses and heals sick parts humans caused but cannot heal on her own.

Then do you mean in the case of Japan too it needs to be washed through natural disaster?

In many cases a region with a lot of natural disasters is usually where their ancestors have accumulated a lot of karmic debts, or because a its location where it was inevitable for them to build up karma. Nature washes down their karma to repay their karma for them.

What karmic debts are you talking about?

Japan invaded and plundered other countries from the ancient times because they couldn't find their position on their own. They fought and killed even each other and so have a history of incessant wind of blood. We can see that there is a big difference when we compare its history to that of neighboring countries.

There were many wars among local lords as seen in western feudalism. Because of the trend of the public that belittles human life and regards suicide as an honor, they left huge karma. That karma was fully transferred to their descendants, but their descendants also immersed themselves in plundering or exploiting others to avoid natural disaster caused by karma, which brought the adverse result of only piling up even more karmic debts.

Besides the places which are known to the public, is there any place that has the potential danger of volcanic eruption?

There are many unknown areas in Japan that have the potential danger of volcanic explosion. From southern Kyushu all along the eastern coast there is a chance of huge damage. Particularly damage from tsunamis will be very serious. Mt. Fuji has less possibility than that, but it also has a chance of explosion.

We are most concerned about year 2012. What do you expect for the condition of natural disasters in that year to be?

You can see earthquakes and volcanic activities will take place almost all over Japan in the Year 2012. In the case of volcanoes, there is a chance that those that already exploded will erupt again. Also strong typhoons will impose a lot of damage on Japan a lot of damage with strong wind and heavy rain. There is a high possibility that huge damage will be incurred on the middle part, Middle Eastern region, and the North Eastern region of Japan. Afterwards it is likely that typhoons and localized heavy rain will follow and sweep the entire nation. If so, they will suffer from a lot of damage by volcanic ash due to aftershocks and the aftereffect of volcanic activities at the end of the year.

Korea

What are the prospects for abnormal climate changes and natural disaster in Korea in 2011?

Due to its location, latitude and geological location where the continent and the sea meet, the damage from the rainy season and cold weather will get more serious. The change of sea currents will bring about fundamental change even in the marine ecology system, and as a result, both the farming and the fishing industry will face a big crisis. Economic difficulty caused by it will hit common people. They will have a depressing summer with a long rainy season, cold weather, a few strong earthquakes and tidal waves to come in the Pacific coast areas.

From the first half of the year even before the rainy season arrives, much rain cloud will rush in, and it will make people feel that it is a completely different climate than before. This kind of weather is the result of the energy of North Pole that got even colder and the energy of the equator that became even hotter getting unstable and often colliding with each other. The air will lose its ordinary direction even more and show instability. The intensity and the area of influence of the cold continental high pressure surrounding the Korean Peninsula will change, therefore spring weather will change totally and summer will get even hotter. There will be much more cloudy days, so naturally the amount of sunshine will decrease.

Because of abnormal climate changes with extremely cold weather and extreme heat, repeated heavy rain and drought, the big crisis of food will double. Years 2010 and 2011 are just the sign of it and it will get even more serious in the future. It is such an obvious situation that even a mere child can know if you open your eyes just a little bit and look at the world.

What can you anticipate from the second half of 2012?

From around the end of 2012, it will be a year that will be dominated by gigantic diastrophism. To begin with the sky will turn ash grey and the sunshine will be blocked for a considerable time period. It is very likely that Korea will be hit by huge tidal waves, the after effect of crustal movement. When it comes to the southern provinces, it is expected that the damage from tidal waves will be more severe as the bed rock sinks down.

One fortunate thing for Korea is that the Japanese islands block tidal waves to a considerable degree. The Taebaek Mountains along the eastern coast and many other mountains will protect many human lives from damage by tidal waves. However, those who live in the Yeongnam region (the south eastern area) and near the rivers in the southern provinces must evacuate. Mostly the Yeongnam region along the southern coast, especially Gyeongnam province will experience severe damage.

The Crisis of the Americas: North America

The Americas are the continents of the western hemisphere that refer to the North and South Americas. The American continents are connected by the Isthmus of Panama. In

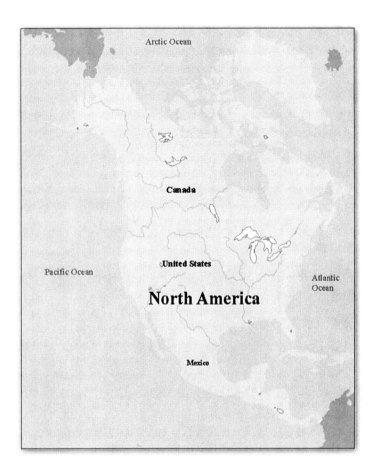

accordance with the ratio of the population, North America is called Anglo America whereas the South is called Latin America. Its size is about 42.0000 km² It accounts for 8.3% of the Earth's surface and 28.4% of the land area. The population is about 900 million (in 2008), that is about 13.5% of the entire world's population.

The United States will be hugely damaged by flooding, tsunami or hurricanes. Most of the causes of why the Earth will have to endure harsh temperatures of down to -40 degrees Celsius will come from Canada. A dreadful chill will hover all over the Earth.

There are many forecasts regarding natural disasters to come to the US such as mega-scale volcanic eruption, tsunamis, earthquakes. What kinds of disasters will hit the US in 2011?

> In 2011, earthquakes will cause huge structural damages to the eastern coast, and many people will be injured or will die. Flooding and tornados will wipe away many crops in the Midwest, and fires will burn on and on in the dry west. 2011 is not the year when they will have huge volcanic eruptions, but volcanoes are accumulating liquefied energy and in the near future they will erupt.

On the East Coast, if it's an earthquake, it will be along the Boston to Washington stretch. Am I correct?

> You are correct.

Are the nuclear reactors in America safe?

> They are not. They are still trying to avoid the lessons from the nuclear fall-out in Japan. It's time to close down the power plants. The coming earthquakes, which will be followed by tsunamis, will rupture parts of the nuclear reactors. It's best to try to close them down now. The entire power grid system of America will be shut down by natural disasters.

What about the southeast of America?

> Tremendous hurricanes will hit Florida and all the states in this region, along with powerful rain storms in the south of America. Due to the logging and denuding of the trees in the Ozark and Appalachian Mountains, the top soil has been removed and dangerous landslides will occur.

The thought just hit me about fires in the West. Forest fires are very hard to control in the dry, desert parts of the West. Will we also see raging fires?

Yes, they will appear. They will go out of control and will approach the cities. They will be handled, but there will be little rain this year in California, so the parched land will be ripe for fires. There are no easy solutions for humans.

Schools of fish, seals and birds appear in mass-suicides almost every day in America. Why is this?

It's telling you to wake up to the condition of the earth and to make a change in your policies and behavior, which will hopefully reduce the size of the natural disasters to come.

What can we expect from 2012?

In terms of national disasters, we will see severe storms, like hurricanes attack the coastal areas, wiping out huge tracts of land and homes. Similar to Hurricane Katrina, major coastal cities will be flooded out. The effects of Peak Oil will set in, and we will see the energy grids affected. Power outages will be longer and will be sustained. Towards the end of 2012, there will be the rumblings of volcanic activity in Montana and Washington states.

These disasters are not set in stone?

Natural disasters are set to come, but their magnitude will depend on the awakening of the American people and the government. It is up to you to now put policies into place to protect nature, its rivers, forest and its animals. The injustice against nature and its animals is an injustice against the Universe itself.

What about Canada. I think they will be similarly affected?

Canada will be affected by earthquakes in the West and by volcanic activity, but there will be less damage in Canada. Their karmic history is one of the cleanest in the West. Similarly, they will suffer from deadly hurricanes along the east coast and from tornadoes and floods in the prairie areas, which will destroy their crops. Canada will gradually enter a freezing ice period. The rising sea levels will increase the soil erosion and landslides along the British Colombia coasts. Canada will go through extreme blizzards in the winters and extreme fires in the summer months.

The nature of Canada should, when we ruminate on the meaning of the vast territory it holds on the Earth, have been preserved; especially the forest and trees. Nevertheless, it is the world's No. 1 paper exporter, and this is the evidence that shows they have forgotten about their task on the Earth. The aftermath will be transferred to the entire Earth, in the same way that the disappearing rain forests of the Amazon does...

In the dimension of the whole Earth, the Canadian Tundra forest should have been protected. Now it has been damaged and from their territory conjunct to the North Pole, an enormous quantity of chilled energy will come down and disasters due to the cold will begin.

Most of the causes why the Earth will have to endure harsh temperatures of down to -40 degrees Celsius will be provided by Canada. A dreadful chill will hover all over the Earth.

When will it happen?

Even though there are some variables, the winter of 2012 will probably be the pinnacle of the coldness.

The Crises of Central and South America

Now let us talk about the natural disasters that will arrive in Central America. I know that Central America is a narrow isthmus, so it's easily affected by the weather storms of the Pacific, Atlantic, Gulf of Mexico and the Caribbean.

Yes, it's a narrow land located at the merging point of many weather patterns, and not only that, but the Pacific plates gather there. These are unstable and cause many volcanic earthquakes.

And due to the poverty and misuse of the land, the number of people who will die or who will be badly affected by disasters is very high in this region.

Yes, this is one of the worst regions for natural disasters and the damage it causes.

What type of natural disasters will we see in 2011?

El Salvador will continue to see water levels rising along the coast and a series of earthquakes. But overall, we will see the threat of volcanic activity from Guatemala down to Panama. Heavy rains will pour down and as the soil has been eroded from intensive farming, we will see many landslides, and the land will begin to slip away. Many poor people will be swept away along with their poorly constructed houses. All of this will affect the crops for exports as well as the local crops for subsistence.

What about in the northern area?

Mexico, especially the Yucatan will be targeted by hurricanes. Hurricanes you cannot imagine will begin to terrorize the Yucatan peninsula down to Honduras.

Then what will happen in 2012?

Depending on how people wake up in 2011 the degree of natural disasters will be decided, but overall they will be much stronger than 2011. For example, 2011 will be the year of rains and floods, but 2012 will the year the grounds starts to shake and fire starts to burst from the mountains. Shaking, rumbling and rocking.

As people run out of their food, water and energy, they will fall into confusion. From 2012, dangerous natural disasters will emerge; especially in cities. Civil war could possibly break out, or just over-all chaos.

Even war with nearby countries could happen over water, rice, or oil. If the response of human beings is not correct, we will see a major break down in the governmental system and economy.

What will be the natural disasters in 2011 in South America?

They have already begun. We are seeing the earthquakes in Chile, the droughts in the N. West, including in the Amazon, and flooding in Brazil. It will be hard to find potable water and energy shortages will become more frequent as the glacial icebergs melt and the dams dry up. There will be major rationing of water and energy. The people will feel angry due to inflation and rationing. Diseases will spread.

What will be the immediate effect?

At first only the poor will protest and it will be ignored by the international community, and the governments will try to pass the blame. However, the middle class will soon begin to dwindle as they join the ranks of the poor. All of a sudden, the number of people in the poor class will increase and will begin to protest.

How will the land formation change in South America?

We are not sure at the moment but it looks like a split will happen and the continent will be divided, it will actually drift away or go under water. It is likely that the affected areas will be in the South western part.

The Crisis of Africa

The continent is located in the South West side of the Eastern Hemisphere, and is the second biggest continent. The equator crosses along its center so that it has tropical and subtropical climates. Its size is 30,200,000 km^2, that covers 6% of the Earth's surface.

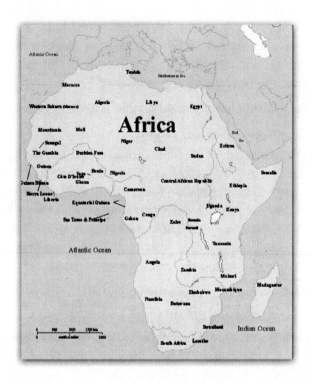

It accounts for 14.8% of the world's population. On this continent, there are 54 countries. Most of them are in poverty and need food support from developed countries. However, the rations are so small that many people starve or are malnourished.

In 2011 and 2012, Africa will experience more climatic variation and extreme weather events than ever before. Also, due to them, it will suffer from food shortages, diseases and social unrest.

I heard there could be some major changes in the next few years. What can we expect to happen in Africa?

Drought and flooding are already causing difficulties in Africa as they always have, however the intensity of the droughts and floods over the next couple of years are going be serious beyond your imagination. Africa will experience more climatic variation and extreme weather events than ever before.

Electrical Storms in Southern Africa will intensify to the point of being dangerous to human life, more intense tropical cyclones will develop off the Eastern Coast of Africa, rainfall will vary so much that it will be impossible to accurately predict how the weather will be in terms of food production. Even though Africa will get progressively drier, there is the likelihood of a higher frequency of intense downpours, which will create flooding in new areas.

North African Countries are on the boundary of the African tectonic plate and are set to experience not only profound earthquakes but also tsunamis. The major cities in northern Africa are built on an active fault system that has a strong potential for a serious earthquake, and the loss of life in these megacities will be in the hundreds of thousands. Survivors won't be many, and the surrounding desert area will be completely unable to support life by then, as it would have become drier and drier. All the deserts in Africa will become much drier and totally uninhabitable and even larger than they are now.

Coastal water levels will rise as the level of the oceans rise and this will have devastating consequences for the Nile Delta and parts of West Africa will be completely submerged. Many people in West Africa would find themselves stuck between the sea and the vast desert with no food or water. So, people will have to move south in order to survive. The Southern part of Africa would be less affected by this, as the altitude is higher. Therefore there will be masses of west- African refugees spreading into central and Southern Africa.

It is expected that North Africa will be uninhabitable by 2015 – it will be completely devoid of human, plant and animal life.

East Africa is going to experience severe Earthquakes. East Africa will also be affected by desertification as the droughts there worsen and central Africa's forests and plains are likely to experience devastating fires. Most likely there will be so many people crowded around the great lakes in central / eastern Africa as the sources of fresh water will be few and there will be many refugees from West and North Africa too. As people crowd around the sources of fresh water in central Africa however, there is another disaster related to the underground volcanic movements waiting to happen there. Under some of those lakes there are huge pockets of volcanic gas, like carbon dioxide. When the volcanic activity begins, there is a high possibility that the gas pockets could be disturbed and release in a limnic eruption.

(Note: A limnic eruption occurs when a gas, usually CO_2 suddenly erupts from deep lake water, posing the threat of suffocating wildlife and humans all around. Such an eruption may also cause tsunamis in the lake as the rising gas displaces water and it happens with no warning at all.)

Many African people are already poor and malnourished which places them at a greater risk for disease. I am wondering about the effect of all this flooding on the health and wellbeing of the people...

Africa is more vulnerable to diseases that most other continents. It is partially because there are many lethal bacteria and viruses present on the continent and also because poverty has become very common.

The deadly infectious diseases can easily be released by changes in weather patterns because they can be picked up by water during times of flooding and can also be carried by human beings and animals which are fleeing natural disasters, such as flooding or fires. As we will certainly see an increase in natural disasters over the next 2 years, we can also expect outbreaks of diseases that you have not encountered or named before and for which there are no medical defenses set up. Due to the number of climate refugees expected, which always entail poor living conditions, poor nutrition and unhygienic living conditions, Africa could experience much loss of life due to disease outbreaks alone in the next few years.

The Crisis of Europe

Europe is surrounded by the Arctic Ocean to the north, by the Atlantic Ocean to the west and by the Mediterranean Sea to the south, and divided from Asia to its east by the Ural Mountains, the Ural River, the Caspian Sea, the Caucasus Mountains, the Black Sea and the Bosporus. Europe can be divided into Western Europe, Northern Europe, Central Europe, Southern Europe and Eastern Europe. Its population is about 790 million, the second largest one to that of Asia. Its population density is about 70 persons/km², lower than that of Asia but over 20 times that of Oceania, and almost 2 times that of the world. Europe is one of the most highly populated areas in the world.

There will probably be a variety of natural disasters due to abnormal climatic changes. Cold waves and drought are expected in the northern part of Europe. Floods and heavy snowfalls will happen seasonally in the central and western regions. The danger of the eruption of Italian volcanoes in the Alpine orogenic zone is highly probable and the volcano in Iceland is also highly likely to erupt.

Natural disasters have already begun in Europe too. It seems that there will more severe natural disasters in the coming years. What causes such disasters to take place in Europe?

In the case of Europe, we can say the karmic debts people have accumulated are one of the biggest causes. Since the dawn of history, the countries in Europe have got material wealth and stability through their innumerable wars and invasions of other countries. Therefore, it is a matter of course that they have accumulated huge karma.

Many European countries made colonies, took advantage of and plundered other countries for their own material abundance. On the contrary, they did not treat the people of the countries equally at all. It is their problem that they racially discriminated against other people and trampled down their rights for their own wealth and happiness. How could human beings do such things to other human beings? A little more thought would have made them know that they could not do so. With love in their hearts, how could they have ignored others' sufferings?

As Europeans' hearts are not as developed as their heads due to their characteristics, they might be somewhat insensitive to such things. But that can be said to have contributed to the behavior and history which demonstrates a lack of basic respect and understanding for human beings.

Human behavior and mind can be described in terms of energy. From that viewpoint, we can say that Europe has scattered much negative energy all over the Earth. Such energy does not just disappear but comes around again after remaining there for a while. Generally speaking, when one oppresses or plunders others with physical force, such actions hurts their feelings and are accumulated in them as emotions such as grudges, hatred, sorrow and regret. After some time the energy of such accumulated emotions will return directly or indirectly to the person who caused them. That is why Europe will suffer more severe natural disasters and starvation than any other area in the coming years.

It is pitiful from the viewpoint of humanity, however it is quite a natural process in the circulating principles of nature. Thus, it is necessary to deal and co-exist with people or nature based on principles and on reason.

I would like to know about the natural disasters that Europe will go through in the years of 2011 and 2012. Recently floods, heavy snowfalls, cold waves and a volcanic eruption took place successively in Europe. What kinds of disasters can we expect to happen in Europe in the future?

There will probably be a variety of natural disasters due to abnormal climatic changes. Cold waves and droughts are expected in the northern part of Europe. Floods and heavy snowfalls will happen seasonally in the central and western regions. The danger of the eruption of Italian volcanoes in the Alpine orogenic zone is highly probable and the volcano in Iceland is also highly likely to erupt. It is not that only one type of disaster will happen in one distinct area, but natural disasters human beings can hardly predict will arise according to seasons and to the situations of the Earth.

Do you mean that abnormal climate will make it difficult to grow crops and that the prices of grains will rise greatly, without exception?

Yes, I do. When they have a poor harvest of crops and the grain prices soar, it will be very hard to raise livestock. It will become hard to get cheese or other dairy products that Europeans enjoy. It is not reasonable to breed animals when people do not have enough food to eat.

Also, as wheat can't be stored for a long time in a humid climate, Europeans will have more difficulty than people who live on rice. Even worse, it is expected that they will have to struggle in hardship since they also will not have meat or dairy products.

How will such phenomena come about in 2012?

The areas such as the hills in central Europe, the low lands of France and the plains in Germany will be damaged by droughts or floods and it will be difficult to grow crops there. Britain and Ireland are not free from disasters either. Such island countries will suffer from tsunamis and storms, or from heavy snowfalls and rainfalls, and will also be affected by the earthquake waves of the Atlantic Ocean.

Besides many natural disasters that will happen all over the continent, earthquakes hit seriously. Then the people who will already be seized with fear will be even more terrified. Unlike other natural disasters, earthquakes can turn everything into ruins in an instant. A great number of casualties are anticipated from earthquakes. In 2012, Europe will be the place where even though people make every effort for survival, they won't find a way.

Part 4

Chapter 9

The New Humankind of the 5th Dimension

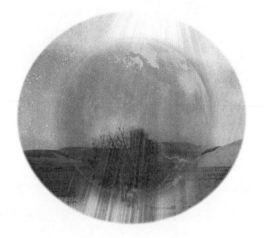

The Secret of the New Humankind's Ether Body

Today I'd like to ask about how human beings will be transformed from the 3rd dimension to the 5th dimension.

All living beings on the Earth will be changed after the Earth's great change. Which topic would you like to start with?

Firstly, I wonder how the human body will be structured after the great change.

At the atomic level, the structure of the human body, which used to be in the 3rd dimension, will be changed to accept the 5th dimension. Molecules will be made into new structures, and DNA will expand from the current 1 pair strand to 6 pair strands in order to fully accommodate the human body, mind and spirit. As the structure and arrangement of organs are changed, the body's sensory ability will expand from 5 senses to 10 senses. In other words, the human body that will pass through the photon belt will be restored to its original DNA structure through the process of adapting to and surviving the photon belt.

The human body having been reborn like this will have the ability to accept both the material world and the spiritual world simultaneously. It will even have the characteristics of both material (physical body) and ether, and thus it can be called a semi-ether body.

The Mysteries of 6 Pairs of DNAs

-An Antenna to the Universe

Wow, just unbelievable! According to books written by cosmic beings and channelers, human DNA originally used to consist of six pairs of DNA strands, which have been reduced to one pair. Is this right?

Yes, it is. Human DNA originally had the structure of six strands which could maintain oneself in the semi-ethereal state. As you can know from the records prior to Noah in the Bible, the people of the time could live to be almost one thousand years old. Though such things are handed down orally like myths because they weren't documented, they were true. The people could live so long because they had the immunity and life force of the semi-ethereal state with six strands of DNAs.

What made the six pairs of strands of DNAs reduce to only one pair?

Originally human beings had six strands of DNA so they could accept and receive the waves of the Universe as they were and lead their lives close to nature in a pure state. But due to relying on materials, they drifted away from nature.

Do you mean that the DNA itself, that is, the whole body, acted as an antenna to communicate with the Universe?

Basically, yes. As people could transmit and receive energy and information with the Universe automatically through DNA and chakras, which played such roles, they could stay in their best condition there without tissues getting old or sick as they do now. Human bodies were assimilated to the flow of nature and the flow of the Universe, and were equipped for the conditions which enabled them to live a natural life.

The Smart Life Information System

Would you please explain the DNA changes in detail?

Compared to computers, DNA is an integrated system of hardware and software. It processes and stores a large amount of information concerned with all life activities. It also has the self-reproducing ability to breed and maintain its species. So it can be said to be an automated system which can always restore its original healthy life force for itself.

In addition, human beings do not only have a body, i.e., the material of the 3rd dimension but also mental ability with a soul combined with the body. Thus we can say that human DNA was created to process such physical and spiritual functions.

Since the DNA of the present one-pair structure processes all the functions, it has extremely limited functionality compared to the original six strand set. That is to say, their original spiritual and physical functions are greatly reduced. Due to the reduced information processing ability of the DNA, only a very small part of the comprehensive functions of the brain became available to be used. This is interconnected with the reduction of the chakras' functions.

The Connector to the Unseen World

Then, why does the New Humankind need six pairs of DNA in its structure?

The visible material world is less than 1% of the Universe. The vast majority of the Universe is the unseen world that is comprised of waves. To facilitate a passable information process, the minimum level of basic DNA structure as a universal being who can get connected to the unseen world of waves and receive and process its information, should be 6 pairs.

Most of six pairs of the DNA send and receive the Universe's information. They process it by decoding immediately and selecting the necessary ones. The present human DNA of one pair also has the same function. However, modern science has revealed only a part of its function, those dealing with the physical aspects of human beings. People don't know much about the functions of DNA that is connected to the unseen world that belongs to the realms of energy, and spirituality.

A soul's information perception ability and information storing ability are rather the ability to get interlocked to the storage of the Universe, deciphering and recognizing it than that of an individual. We can say that the DNA system the New Humankind will obtain is a system with this functionality; information, which is received through all the senses of the body, is automatically input to the database of the Universe through one's individual DNA system. When necessary, through the linking-up system of chakras and DNA, the information is immediately searched in the database of the Universe and decoded. At last, the New Humankind can display the infinite power and ability of the Universe, that includes the functions of a human and a god combined.

Chapter 10

Chakras' Restoration

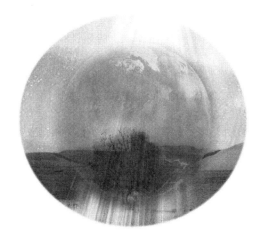

A Chakra is a Relay Station of Information and Energy

What is a chakra and what are its functions?

A chakra is a relay station that receives and transmits information and energy to the places that need it. On the other hand, DNA acts as a terminal console. It is a system like an antenna which has the characteristics of receiving, decoding and recording various kinds of life activities and information. In other words, DNA can be a database of basic programs and information to store, connect and operate high dimensional information of the Universe in order to make use of them.

A chakra is the device for connecting with the networks of the Universe, based on the database of such programs and information. The brain has the function of a command center to make comprehensive decisions by gathering and analyzing such information. Chakras exist as information and energy stations to synthesize and store a large amount of information and energy, to classify them according to function, and to receive and send them.

I took some time to research some information on the functions of chakras. I see they are explained differently in each source. Why is that?

All the acupuncture points of the human body have the function of chakras to some degree. Since the human body, a so-called micro-cosmos, is a huge collection of information itself, it is difficult for even cosmic beings to explain all of its mysteries. Also, acupuncture points have different degrees of awakening in accordance with what levels of information and energies they send and receive and by what dimensions of energies they are connected to.

The system of chakras mentioned by cosmic beings or by Indian yogis in existing books will differ a lot from that of the human beings of the forth coming age of the New Humankind. You may take the information from them just as a reference.

The Essential Chakra Called the "Danjeon"

I became curious about why the devices to receive and transmit the information and energies of the Universe are necessary in the body of human beings who live in the material world.

The human body is not just a simple material being, but it is like a sacred shrine that accommodates a soul; the seed which is the incarnation of the Creator. Therefore, human bodies should be equipped with networking

devices which can connect with the main body of the Universe so that the soul can stay and grow there; chakras are such devices. Also, chakras develop the soul by maximizing the abilities given while human beings have their body through networking between the soul and its body as well as with the Universe.

If so, which chakra has the most essential function amongst the many chakras of the body to move on to the New Humankind?

Of all the human chakras, it is the "danjeon[1]", which is an energy reservoir situated in the lower abdomen of a trainee who practices the danjeon breathing method. The danjeon that acts as the foundation for the power of mind that enables the seed of incarnation of the Creator to germinate and lead the process of becoming one with the essence of the Universe.

If you strengthen your danjeon and enlarge it through breathing, your mind power will be reinforced, and

---

[1]An energy reservoir in a breathing trainee's body is an energy vessel invisible to physical eyes and one can form and grow one's danjeon through practicing danjeon breathing. One builds his danjeon on his own with materials sent from the Universe. It is also called the vessel that accommodates the mind. It is situated at the very center of one's body; the location is a bit different depending on individuals, but roughly 5cm below one's naval.

even your power to accelerate the evolution of the Universe so that you can attain Il-che-yu-shim-jo (Everything is created by the mind.) even after you enter the Universe after taking off your physical body. This is the very power of the danjeon.

The Principles of Transforming into a Different Dimension

Now I would like to know about the principles of human beings changing into a new dimension. According to theosophy, not only the physical body of the third dimension but also the bodies of various dimensions are overlapped in a human body. Would you please explain that?

You may understand the word "ether" as just another expression of the word "gi (energy; ki or qi in Japanese or Chinese pronunciation)". As mentioned in theosophy, it can be said that the physical body and gi body (ethereal body) exist together overlapped in a body. Because the human body assumes the condition where a spiritual being wears a physical body, it has to take such a dual structure.

Nonetheless, such a gi body (ethereal body) is a being beyond the material, 3rd dimension, so it may be perceived not to exist in the 3rd dimension. It is understood to be just a phenomenon which responds to the materials of the 3rd dimension and is manifested.

All dimensions have their own dimensional walls. Everything is a real existence within the same dimension. But when a dimension shifts, the beings of the 4th dimension, for example, are perceived not to exist in the 3rd dimension.

The 4th dimension exists overlapped in the atmosphere of the Earth, but people can't perceive its existence at all in the 3rd dimension; so it becomes the story of another world. Though the worlds of different dimensions exist overlapped in the same time and space, they exist independently without any interruption to the world of another dimension.

Because things exist in different form depending on dimensions, it is impossible to observe another dimensional world from a 3rd dimensional world without having a special ability to transcend dimensional walls. As mentioned above, you can only observe another dimension to a certain extent through the phenomena that reacts to the materials of one's own dimension.

Conversations through waves beyond time and space like ours, spiritual phenomena, usually referred to as telepathy, scalar waves which scientists are talking about these days, anti-matter and so on – all of these are phenomena existing across dimensions.

A Semi-etheric Body

I understand. In what state are semi-ether bodies? Please explain more specifically.

Semi-ethereal bodies can show the characteristics of the physical bodies of the present 3rd dimension and of the ether bodies of the 5th and above dimensions at the same time. This is a kind of transitional state before physical bodies become complete ether bodies. Although they have the physical body of the 3rd dimension, they have the characteristics close to those of an ether body as the ether body of the 5th dimension is activated. In other words, the present people on the Earth have limited functions because their ether body is subordinated to their physical body of the 3rd dimension. In the state of a semi-ether body, the functions of their bodies get close to those of an ether body.

When we, humans, are etherealized, will the Earth itself be etherealized too? Or will only the people on the Earth be etherealized while the Earth remains in its state of the material?

Although I cannot know all the schedules of the Universe, I think the Earth will also be in the semi-ether state where materials and ether can co-exist.

It has been mentioned that there are ten dimensions in the Universe. Beings in the 5th dimension exist in the semi-ether state and exist in a full ether state in the dimensions above that.

That's right. However, all the ether bodies are not the same. The ether bodies of different dimensions take on different aspects of existence. That's because of the difference of waves. The finer one's wave is, the more information and abilities it contains. In the world of higher dimensions, various conditions become possible that don't exist in the lower dimensions and there are various phenomena which cannot be perceived in the lower dimensions.

The lower a being's dimension is, the more distinctive individuality its body-form has. On the other hand, beings of higher dimensions can have a variety of bodies according to their need or exist in the states which are closer and closer to light without being bound in a certain body-form. I think, very high dimensional beings exist in the state of emptiness, like the Creator, ultimately.

I really appreciate all of this beautiful information you gave me today.

The Life of the New Humankind

I would like to ask you about how this society would change after the Earth passes through the photon belt. Before we start our conversation in earnest, I think we need to roughly outline the Earth circumstances after the Earth passes through the photon belt. What do you think?

That sounds good. I guess it would be nicer if we build some understanding about the overall issues so that we can talk deeply about politics, which will be the main topic of our conversation.

Thank you! Okay, then would you talk a little bit about the Earth passing through the photon belt?

The Earth might pass through the photon belt around the beginning of 2013. Of course there are some variables. Before the Earth passes through the photon belt, it will go through terrible disasters. There won't be any people who do not suffer from the Earth's situation. Pains and wounds will be dominant all over society. The public authorities will be vulnerable regarding them. When you enter the photon belt in that situation, it means the end of Earth's civilization that has dominated the world. Also it is the sign that tells you that a new era has arrived. Yet, the beginning of new world is not only bright or hopeful. Life will be very severe. After you have spent a long painful night and get to a new day, then humankind will start moving slowly in order to continue living their lives.

After the Earth passes through the photon belt, what will happen? What will happen exactly in terms of the Earth's climate and purification activity?

Just as it takes some time for humans to adapt to a new environment, the Earth also needs to take its time. While the Earth is preparing for a dimension change, it will wriggle a lot, and during the period of adjustment to a new world, you will still have many natural disasters.

However, the frequency will diminish soon. If you get through the year 2013 well, everything will improve after that.

How many public facilities, airports, roads or highways will be damaged while the Earth suffers from natural disasters and passes through the Photon Belt?

The damage will be different for each country, but roads and highways of most countries will be destroyed so you won't be able to use them. Disconnected parts will appear frequently so that roads won't fulfill their roles.

So will airports and other facilities. You know human-made buildings are so feeble even now. They will hardly remain the same when they are hit by natural disasters. Not all facilities will be destroyed but it will take a lot of time to build them all over again.

Especially countries that have been hit by earthquakes often will be fatally damaged. Countries on the circum-Pacific belt such as Japan or Australia will require dozens of years or several hundred years before they recover fully.

What about communication facilities?

They are the same. Even if they remain safe from natural disasters, most devices will become of no use as they go through the photon belt.

Well... I heard that the Earth will meet a great solar storm by May of 2013. I heard electronic products will be affected or

will be out of order by it. Will they also be influenced by the photon belt? Even before the Earth is hit by a solar storm...?

Yes. The photon belt is a cosmic ray. Cosmic rays are electromagnetic waves as well as scalar waves that bring about changes in biological energy. When the Earth passes through the photon belt, they will be frequently influenced by electromagnetic waves whose wavelengths are short and exposed to the influence. Also, since the magnetism will stop functioning for a while, enormous amount of cosmic rays will fall down on the Earth. Accordingly, sensitive electronic devices will be critically ruined.

I doubt whether public municipalities will be able to do their work well when the traffic and communications don't work, and when people suffer from food and water, shortages, it will become difficult for people to adapt to a new environment after the Earth passes through the photon belt. You know, for example, what about public servants, the police or army?

Many social systems will collapse. First of all, there won't be many survivors, thus any kind of system won't work well. Even if a president commands something, there won't be enough people who can carry it out because those who play their role of linking in systems are missing.

Then what could people do to restore a minimum level of activities in order to get supplies of food and water, even if there aren't many people?

A couple of people who survive will carry out such activities voluntarily and in a self-governing way. In each local region, those who have their roles will move to carry on their roles and they will strive for their survival and restoration focused on the survivors.

However, there won't be many things for them to do. People will try to supply food, water and medicine. The necessary activities for survival will be carried out.

Today's conversation reminds me of a disaster movie. I feel depressed.

Well, I would like to tell you something more optimistic but some good news will come out after we will talk about disasters

O.K., I see. Let me continue to talk then. After passing the photon belt, when the restoration work begins based on local villages, won't they form small-sized self-governing communities?

Yes. From the bottom level, spontaneous groups will come to existence, and will begin the restoration process. Some of the previous organizations with functions will begin re-activating and focusing on people with their own roles of expertise, the groups will become systemized. Sufficient locomotion is not available, so people will have movements and form organizations on a small, local scale.

When will municipalities or local authorities become active in order to maintain social order?

All the social order will remain destroyed and all system will be paralyzed, but it will take a long time for a minimum level of service to be restored. That is because efforts to recover the system will be made from many angles during the year 2013. Of course the chaos will last because there will be a number of casualties. Anyway, the world will get back to a normal state little by little.

At this time, the roles of those who are awakened will really matter. They need to find out what the message of terrible disasters is and reflect on where humankind is heading, analyze the reasons of those disasters and they should be able to present alternative ways to the world. At this time, alternative ways of living for the New Humankind will be magnified to be very important. Depending on how those people show their leadership to recover from the chaos, the period needed to handle it will decrease.

Then would the world be restored to as it is now? Then would nothing be different from now?

No, it is not so. Of course people would try to go back to their previous lifestyle. Yet, out of enormous mental confusion they will have no option but to admit that they need some changes and they will listen to alternatives so as not to return to the past. Humanity will open up their eyes about their situation sometimes through the form of cosmic beings' voices or heavenly messages.

A new system will be created in order to lead a new world. In the beginning, even though people will try to restore things to a similar way to the previous system; at this point it will be necessary to present alternatives to people in more active ways, and the vision regarding the new civilization will play such an important role.

Hmm...it sounds a bit vague. Do you mean nothing is settled yet and things will differ depending on what we suggest to people?

Let me tell you more specifically. First of all, most social systems will be paralyzed by tremendous disasters and changes. Lines will be cut off and communications will be blocked. Everywhere people will suffer from starvation and disease. After some time, people will voluntarily make efforts to survive. The movement to survive will begin by each local community where people can communicate with each other. Communication means will be connected again but due to the disconnection of transportation, the transportation of goods won't be easy for some time.

In this restoration period, what will function will be the decision-making bodies in local communities, and local authorities such as public offices, police, public servants and the army will take actions little by little. When they are connected nationwide, people will try to restore the previous social system. In this process if there are no actions by those who are awakened, they will try to restore them in completely inefficient ways, and moreover in a way which reverts back to the past system.

Therefore, you need to explain the causes that bring about such disasters and some alternative ways of living. The alternative way of living with regard to food, energy and medicine should be accepted by people. It won't be difficult to persuade people because you cannot find solutions if you get back to the old way.

Have you ever experienced them? On your planet or in another planet where you once lived?

Ha ha ha! I am sorry but I have never experienced them.

I see, but you describe all those things as if you had experienced them as far as I receive your message correctly.

Well, I did not experience such disasters in person but such situations are easily found in the history of the Universe. So as a matter of fact we can't understand the pains Earth people are going through 100%, but since we can learn about the course from other planets' cases in detail, we can give you people of the Earth advice.

The experience the Earth is having now is the course where you can attain such a high level of growth because it is a course with an enormously high level of difficulty from the viewpoint of the evolution process. A person becomes mature through suffering hurt from those that they love and through the birth pangs a new life is born. This pain becomes the foundation where humankind can grow into the new dimension. In that sense, I feel very envious of the present Earth people. You are now experiencing some very wonderful events and having lessons that you can rarely have even in the Universe.

I guess you would say, "Oh, my gosh" if you actually have to experience it yourself.

Probably yes. Well... In fact giving advice in my position now and going through it wearing a physical body all have their own advantages and weaknesses; but anyway from my position as a spectator, I envy you.

Hmm, I guess I would have said the same thing to you if I were you. By the way, the new society is meant to have activities based on small-scale local communities naturally, isn't it? Due to troubles such as the decrease in population and the transportation of goods...

Yes, because they can survive only when they do things in that way... Nevertheless, amongst those who survive, some people would still have the momentum of their lives and some will try to exercise their powers. It will be the role of those who become awakened ahead of them to suggest to them the true way where humankind can survive and lead them through conversation with them.

As I read the conversations we had so far, we will meet a totally different society after the Earth passes through the photon belt. Do you mean that a new society will be created from a zero base?

Yes.

Then, would it be useful to talk about new politics?

Politics is a tool that directs a society. Based on collective opinions, you find the best way to evolve a society. The reason that you talk about politics is because you need to think about how you will create a system that can evolve a society.

As you say so, I feel a bit lost about what to ask. As a matter of fact, I prepared some questions regarding the established social systems and politics. You know the problem of democracy, the separation of three powers, and a parliamentary system and so on. In a large sense, I want to ask you about conflicts between countries, wars, and the role of the UN or NGO. Well... as you say the previous political system won't work, so I don't know what to ask you.

Ha ha ha! It is fine. You can ask about them too. It must also be meaningful to talk about such things one by one. They are not meaningless at all for the future political system. I can tell you an ideal political system of an evolved planet but such system won't be introduced for a while. You might need to experience a transitional period. Then you can apply the current political system in the transitional period.

I guess, at that time, the distribution of goods won't be possible because transportation won't be available. What do you think?

You are right. It will take a lot of time until you develop resources and produce goods. Yet, you will bring to an end to the current ways of developing resources and manufacturing goods as they are not desirable. This will be a lesson that the humankind would learn from natural disasters. Yet, an issue of survival will be very critical and urgent, so food, water, medicine and second hand goods will be distributed by a small market.

What will happen to capitalism as an ideology as well as a social system? If goods are distributed only in a small market, it will be hard to regard it as capitalistic system. How can we define this?

The distribution of goods on a small scale has been in human society for a long time. You cannot say this is only a characteristic of capitalism. From the aspect of ideology that rules a society, we can call this capitalism. This is just a small-sized living community that is self-sufficient.

Do you mean a kind of primitive community?

You cannot say it is a primitive community. Even though you will live in a self-sufficient economy, in terms of technology, it will be much more developed than now. Developed technologies from evolved planets will be handed down to people for producing energy and goods. There is a variable regarding when it will be done, though. Depending on what people will restore their civilization with, it will be decided whether cosmic beings will be involved in the restoration work. How much we will be involved or when we will be involved will be made possible depending on how much people make an effort and how much they want. This is also a variable determined by the role of those who are awakened.

As economically self-sufficient communities become revitalized, financial transactions will be done locally. It is a system where local people create alternative currencies that are only used in their local community. This is the currency that will be issued by residents every time they need it; it will function as a means that only improves the exchange of commodities and services. You will see various alternative currencies.

Economic activity based on local communities, the exchange of labor and alternative currencies will all contribute to localization. By exchanging commodities or services, you can enjoy services that a market or a nation cannot provide even if you do not have money. Also activities like those will revitalize local economies as well as local communities.

O.K., I see. I think I can imagine how the economy would turn out now. This time, let's get back to political system again. After the great change, do you think that political parties like you see now will be created? Will a party like the progressive or conservative be significant then?

Ha ha! Parties won't be active anymore after the great change. Some people who used to have power might want to create such a party but since people will be spiritually enlightened at that time, major directions will be decided according to the will of Universe.

Those who survive will become people who understand the Universe. There must be a lot of variables that might occur in the transitional period but the current political system won't be formed again.

The most spiritually evolved and wise person will make important decisions as it is on evolved planets. Such systems will be adopted naturally in a small area and as this will spread to a larger area, so nations and the entire world will be led in this way.

I am getting excited about it. Now let me ask you about an election. When people start to restore a social system after the chaos, a representative will be necessary even if it is a small town. How will this be done?

A process to elect a representative won't be so different from now in terms of its procedure. There will be a person who represents a community, and you need an election process in order to pick out a person who is responsible for the community where you belong. However, a big difference between now and then is that such an election will be made naturally according to each characteristic of the community.

Today's elections are done according to the same standard nationally (a committee member per ten thousand people). In the future, this will be done locally. Representatives that are from each community will form an assembly. Yet, they are not statesmen like today as a profession but rather form a gathering where they can make decisions like the concept of a committee.

Then how will they make decisions? Do they make decisions like now? Currently political leaders first discuss an issue and make decisions by majority.

Well… A political system is not just given automatically. Humans have to create this. It all depends on you. In the new civilization of the New Humankind, everything you think about becomes transparent. Complicated processes, a struggle for power or plotting that you find in the current political system won't be found then. As all things look so transparent, how will such action be possible? Therefore, in the decision-making process, you will have a process to become in tune together but it won't be so difficult or complicated.

In many cases you will come to an agreement naturally. No matter how difficult the problem is, it won't be difficult to decide which is desirable for all. In many cases, opinions of the wisest person will be mostly reflected.

Okay, I can imagine.

As we talk about politics, I think we need to point out the quality of citizens as well as political leaders. When people are spiritually enlightened, will this affect people's viewpoint on politics and their way of election?

Being spiritually enlightened means that it becomes much easier and more accurate to grasp the essence and people become aware of a person's level or character at a glance. You heard that the people's way of thinking and their levels will become obviously evident at a glance when people become semi-ether; and that is the spiritually evolved condition. When the time arrives, it won't be so hard to elect a leader who will represent you, and you won't have to feel regretful about your decision for a couple of years after you choose a wrong politician, as you do now.

Global issues are discussed in the UN now. How will it change in the future? The UN cannot operate effectively when it comes to interests between powerful countries. It is swayed by several powerful countries like the US or China. Especially with regards to environmental issues

such as global warming, the UN has critical limitation where it can't properly control some countries such as the US. How will it change in the future? Would it be possible to create a decision-making system by a unitary state or an organization?

> Yes, of course. The highest decision-making body on Earth that can replace the UN will be created. It won't take so long. After you pass through the great change, meeting with cosmic beings will be something common in your daily life. Just like you hear the news of the world, it will be the norm that you hear about the news of the Universe through cosmic beings and the new information sharing system. Thus, Earth people will need key people who are in contact with cosmic beings. Those people will be representing Earth people like the present UN.

What about your planet? I heard that this is a highly evolved planet and there is a decision-making body in your planet but no one can force others to obey the decisions. Everyone naturally accepts the decisions for their evolution and performs their roles according to the decisions. How can you maintain a society that way?

> That is a very natural culture. Maybe you cannot understand how this is possible because on the Earth you cannot understand what others are thinking and so you find it difficult to communicate with one another. However, would it be rather strange not to accept decisions when they are made through transparent communication and in the communication process, we can have much wiser opinions from someone.

Even if you say so, I guess each person might have a different idea regarding evolution or a different view point toward the same event. For example, even though it was decided to help the Earth for the good of the Universe's evolution, some cosmic beings might think it would be better not to help the Earth directly, in order to give true help to Earth people.

Of course such opinions can be suggested. All ideas can't be unified into one through the decision making process. We cosmic beings all have our own characteristic and difference in thinking; then how would it be possible to create one single opinion?

However, while they exchange their ideas, they can decide what will be good for the whole even though it is not the same as your opinion. Sometimes the majority of people would have different opinions from you, or when something was presented from a higher level, you would just come to accept the thing you can't understand yet.

You mean there is something like a level difference?

Yes. You can understand that is a process of politics as well as that of high-quality decision making.

The meaning of your politics seems very different from what we have now, like a few people out of those at a similar level are representing the whole and rule over a country.

Yes, therefore you may even say there is no "politics" on advanced planets.

Well, if the Earth can get through a difficult period for a couple of years, the sight of the future looks so hopeful. Maybe it will be a kind of ideal society and ideal politics that humankind has only dreamt about. Maybe in the future philosophers would rule the world as Plato believed.

Yes. The future society will be as ideal as you can imagine now. Diverse opinions and characteristics will be appreciated. All things will be judged by the evolution of the Universe as well as the humankind. That is the first and foremost proposal. Thus in a decision-making process, there won't be big conflicts or clashes. Every single person will be understood and embraced. The decision would be made by a small town and finally the entire planet will make a decision.

The only thing that the new humankind requires is to extensively experience anything that is truly helpful for them to evolve. When you accumulate such experiences, you will expand your wisdom.

The concept of politics won't be like you are opposed to a different party and therefore hold fast to your views. People would understand that everyone is different and they would be concerned for others. Politics will act as a vehicle for sharing experiences with one another. This is an ideal society that Earth's humankind has dreamt about achieving for such a long time.

The future society is not a complete one yet so you will have to solve problems that might occur, but that is how you evolve yourself. This is the same in the planet where I am now. In that sense, we are important partners to each other because we both make an effort to evolve ourselves, which is the great stream of the Universe.

Chapter 11

Society and the Culture After the Earth's Great Change

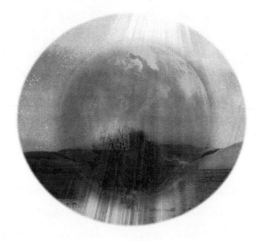

This time, I would like to ask you about society and culture. Because of our previous conversation, I can guess what the story might be like; that the change is in progress to some extent. So it would be great if you can tell me about the story after the change when it has settled down.

By the way... Do you know about everything I am asking you about?

Yes, I do to some degree. But I cannot tell you very specifically. Even though we do have a respectable amount of information, the Earth has an infinite possibility for alteration. Also you are in the situation of exchanging conversations, thus the variables are gradually increasing even more. Therefore, it would be good if you receive answers first, and then examine the alteration of society.

I understand. Now let me give you some questions. I am concerned about the matter of communications and that we might experience some problems after the period of change. The internet sustains contemporary life. How will this change? Is the internet going to remain?

Of course it will. The internet will continuously exist. Even after undergoing the magnetic storm, you will be able to find that some equipment still works.

Looking at the beginning of the internet, the internet was an idea that the Pentagon originated in order to make a reliable communication system even in a nuclear war. Now it has been commercialized, large communication enterprises have emerged and you can communicate with numerous packets of information through an optical LAN. But after the change, there will be small server companies in the neighborhood towns, which will be in charge of communication technology.

Rather than a company, it will more than likely begin as a club activity. As a matter of course, in many respects including the speed of the lines, the service would be difficult to compare to that of the old days, but the decentralization of the communication service will bring many changes in the flow of society's information too.

Well… That might happen. But if there is bunch of communication operators existing in towns, would it be possible for them to function when we have a central

communication operator? Isn't the telephone line or something else necessary to make it work?

The internet is not such a concept. The laptop that you are using right now is capable enough of performing the IDC (internet data center) function. So, there will be small, large, and various size of internet companies.

The core of the SETI (Search for Extraterrestrial Intelligence) project is distributing the function of a super computer into a variety of personal computers, and then processing the advanced mathematical arithmetic operations. Consequently, there will be many concepts like that.

Will pop culture last? Such as the movies for the public, will the leisure culture disappear?

Movies will never die out. Movies will be the last to disappear. However, their form might change a little in time. A movie is a story. Do you think that humans will get bored of stories? The movie industry will survive by all means. Nevertheless, I doubt that there will be investment on a grand scale in movies as there is now. There will be much more creation of contents, but movies will be more like explorations about humans' inner aspects, hence the concept of blockbusters will disappear and move on to the course of a personalized movie service.

Will the movie theatres last?

Yes, they will. They won't change too much. There will be developments in technology, but people will come to watch olden-day movies rather than new movies. While people are watching a movie together, they will enjoy their time recalling the past. The form of the current movie theaters where people only concentrate on watching movies will mostly disappear. A hybrid industry will develop, such as having supper or having tea while watching a movie.

How about the Hollywood system? Will this last? I still love the large-scale movies of Hollywood.

During the period of change, enough various stories will arise, and then so many movies and literary works will appear in order to memorize those days. But, there won't be movies like there are now. The movies that have been watched will now be classified as classic films, and they will be used in the form of the existing media. The new form of movie that will come out, will use the technique of stimulating the nerves; the movies won't include just images but the new style of movies that will be taken that will convey the information to our sense of touch, taste, and even to our sense of smell.

In addition, the movie will be produced as a method of collecting and conveying new images or memories. It won't fictionalize a new story or have someone act out the story; but it will use the method of conveying one's memory as it is. It may be difficult to imagine, but the ascension of the dimension will make this possible.

The Hollywood system is the possible structure when there is a large scale audience. But, such a large scale audience won't be crowding into the movie theaters, thus the current form of movie industry will be difficult to find for a while.

Hmm… It will leave much to be desired. I enjoyed the scale of the Hollywood movies.

It's after going through the hard times… Every day's life will be like a movie, so people won't really want the blockbusters. Their lives will be the blockbuster movie itself.

It may turn out so... but I still feel somewhat bitter.

So then... Why don't we move on to music? What will happen to music?

Music spread through the internet will be the general trend, and there will hardly be any musician playing commercial music. Rather, there will be many people performing their music in order to soothe people's hearts. Musicians will perform music by paying more attention to healing than to stimulating people to earn attention. This is the reflection of the social situation.

Now, sexy and good-looking girl singers are the zest and amusement of people's lives, but at that time, since people will need consolation, courage and hope, other kinds of music will increase. Musicians won't form an industry. Rather, they will focus on communities for their performances. Accordingly, there will be more people who will play music as a hobby than becoming professional musicians. And music will become a part of living, hence the people's latent desire for music will burst out, so more and more people will learn to play musical instruments and sing. Music is the easiest entertainment, isn't it?

It will be possible to use the musical instrument as it is now, so there will be many people enjoying singing and dancing and an orchestra will be formed in each town. Learn how to play at least one musical instrument from now on. Then, you will be quite popular later.

What kind of music will people like?

As time goes by, people will prefer simple sounds. Rather than the chord with many sounds, the simple sound enjoying its purity will become a trend, hence the need for a good voice and an instrument of new tones will increase. Also the music form of choirs and a'cappella will become a main trend. These will lead the musical trends after the period of change.

Oh, I see. Then I will move on to the topic of eating.

Oh, I love to talk about eating. Isn't it one of the top 3 desires of Earth people?

Yes, it is. I wonder, even at that time, if it would be the same as now. Such as, will the coffee brands remain the same as they used to be...

Through the climate change, preserved food will be the general trend in the near future. And coffee won't be easily grown because of the soil. In addition, later when we reach the period of convalescence, people's physical constitution will change, so people won't need so much food.

There will be some areas where you will be able to cultivate coffee, but no one knows if the taste of coffee would be same as now.

Well... Starting the day by having a cup of Cappucino or an Americano at Starbucks is the wish of the salary man. Would it be difficult?

Well, there will be some. But coffee is just a luxury and a favorite food. Because coffee will exist at that time, people will have a special outing like sharing the rare coffee at the coffee shop. Having a coffee will be one of the few dining out experiences.

All right, now, I will move on to love affairs. What will the standard of an ideal type of love affair be? Will this change?

In the early stages, a powerful and muscular guy will be the mainstream. Because the situation during the changing period won't be easy to live out, the man who can protect and has power to pioneer would be an ideal type.

But as society recovers its stability, the man who is good at communication will find himself in favor more and more. The man who is not just farming through strength, the man who communicates with nature and the Universe; understands and loves wounded people's hearts would become an ideal type. Even now, it is like this too; the person who understands one's mind well would be an ideal type.

I see. It is an eternal truth. But the reality is "I don't even understand my mind". If one has an ability to understand another's mind, that would be an outstanding skill.

That's because people don't try to feel. The attitude of trying to commune, trying to know and trying to feel is the basic attitude of love. Just showing and delivering your emotion is the egoistic love only for yourself, it is not the love that communicates. This is applicable even now, so bear this in mind.

Ah... I see. Anyway, I think it is a problem that nowadays people's partners in love change too often. In the future, will the situation be the same?

It will change a bit. The social atmosphere of nowadays is the same all over the world. It is the culture created by the obsession with sex. "How can I get to sleep with her, how can I have new stimulation", people concentrate on these things. That's why they always create the same situation, looking for a new partner and replacing them over and over again.

However, it will be a bit different in the future society. The senses of human beings will be developed without precedent so that even if people are in love with just one person, people would feel much more than they do now, so they will experience a fulfilled feeling of love. It would be same for the sexual engagement as well, people will have the feeling that is several times stronger than the orgasm that current humanity has. People won't even feel the need to look for a new date. On the contrary if one has any negativity towards their partners it will be sensed instantly. The New Humankind will not be able to hide their mind and emotions, let alone cheat in a relationship.

In the beginning, this phenomenon will start with women and this will give men a difficult time, but later men's senses will be slowly awakened as well and will sense women's minds. Then people will be satisfied with just one partner. How long they would continue their relationship will depend on each other, and since they know well that they can't hide anything, they will move on to the direction of evolution before the love cools down.

You won't attract opposite sexes because of loneliness. But since you will live a community life with neighboring friends and colleagues, your life will always be balanced in terms of yin and yang. Consequently, rather than looking for someone to replenish your insufficient yang or yin energy, you will become attracted to the one who has the energy you need out of the Five Elements: Tree, Fire, Soil, Metal and Water. And you are well-aware of which energy deficiency caused you to feel attracted to the person, hence marital harmony and saju[1] will become quite an important study.

I can't wait for such a time. (Wow!) But why will saju or marital harmony become an important study?

First, the saju of each person based on the current I-ching[2] will need to be reformulated because the flow of energy will change. The flow of the Five Elements will change gradually, and so will the sequence of the elements: Tree, Fire, Soil, Metal and Water. Those who can understand and read the flow of the energy will need to re-define saju again, and then it will be established as a new study.

Saju is the first starting point of realizing who you are, therefore the beginning of home education will be parents and family members setting up a plan for the child, referring to the saju of the baby. For now, there are many errors in the interpretation of saju, but after the changing period, you will be able to accurately analyze the disposition a human being is born with through the developed sensibility and the newly developed devices' help. Then the margin of error will decrease greatly.

In addition, it will be possible to check one's condition regarding a change in energy. So it won't be like dividing energy change into 4 or 8 constitutions,

---

[1] Each of one's birth year, month, date and time can be analyzed into a vertically-arranged pair of Chinese characters, which show the energy operation of Heaven and Earth; consequently, one's birth time can be analyzed into eight characters. That is why this is called "Four Pillars and Eight Characters." It is one of the most common arts of Asian Divination.

[2] I-Ching: The science of divination; fortune-telling lore based on the change of heaven and earth energy.

but you will figure out your own body constitution and inclination in the middle of the spectrum that include tens of thousands of changes. You will have customized personal analysis, not a stereotypical saju. For now I can compare this to the measurement of the physical development indicator. When you go to the health club, they analyze your degree of muscle development and the percentage of fat, don't they? In the same manner you can make a plan for your life path to go by analyzing your energy arrangement and choosing whether you will make up the energy factor and change it or reinforcing the factor you are born with and establish your own field. Saju will be the study you will need for setting up this kind of plan.

That is a positive prospect. Leading a life by knowing who I am will bring me happiness. Not wandering here and there without knowing what direction to follow.

Though, you will still be wandering. Finding your way forward is never an easy thing to do. There is always something you can't handle even if you are aware of your characteristics. The course of overcoming it is a life and also evolution. The pains for growth exist everywhere. How rugged the path is will determine the speed of one's evolution.

This time, let me inquire about religion. It is such a vast territory, so I will give you some brief questions. Even though I have so many things I am curious about regarding the past and future of religion on the Earth, let's talk about just the religion after the changing period for now.

I will give you a brief summary. Don't take it as difficult. Religion is just following one's teachings about the unknown world. But in the future, the unknown world will disappear. There will be no religion any more. There will only be study.

The beings who were worshiped as God, will visit again and they will become friends, not God.

The world after death will be disclosed and a study about that world will be established. While studying the Universe, you will build up the concept that death is a journey and a life is just a stopover in the middle of the trip. Therefore, you won't have religions that begin from a leader, but a school where you can share your enlightenment with each other.

In religions, there are the commandments and ethics that each of them has established, right? What will happen to the people who abide by them? I think that even if transparent information will be interchanged, religions that have lasted for thousands of years won't disappear.

They will disappear. But not just disappearing. The people who have had the same belief will study that belief together as learning, not as a religion. Religious people will study about all the components of every religion, such as the Realm of Spirits, angels and gods; and they will live while watching the principles and phenomena through their eyes. There will be learning and sharing based on a thorough understanding, not just a blind trust. The concept of religion will disappear, but religion is the culture that has created history, therefore, it will continue to exist as an important aspect of the culture.

There were many religious wars that were caused when Buddhism, Christianity, Roman Catholicism, Muslim and other religions had conflicts against each other. If the community

culture still exists, wouldn't the conflict between each religion get stronger?

They will live life by practicing the true meaning of religion, so the problems regarding disputes will be solved. When they are in the environment where they can't survive without co-existing together, no single human being will be excluded because they are of a different religion. That was a concept required when they wanted to take away things from others; that is not necessary when we have to share things.

Could a unified religion develop?

It is not that a single, unified religion will come to existence. Instead, the academy where religious groups get together and share information with each other will be established. A single religion that you are thinking of won't appear.

Everyone believes in Newton's law of gravity. Because they can see every object falling down. The study of religion will be tied up with science. When the mystic elements of religion become evident, it won't remain as an object of faith; but it will be the object of study and research so that scientific methodology will be applied and the human beings will grow quickly through getting to know much information about the new world. New study that will integrate spirituality and materials will be established.

All right. For now, let's finish our talk about religion here. There are many areas I would like to investigate, but I think it would be too vast to learn about.

It is possible to have a long talk, but it would be more about the past story than the future to come. Let us finish now. As for the future of religion, it is enough to know that religion will be disappearing in the future. You weren't disappointed with the answers, were you?

Oh, no. It is actually very clear. There is no need to have faith in unseen matters, because you will see the world clearly. This phrase can explain everything. That is very concise. Thank you.

The Conditions for Passing Through the Photon Belt

I'd like to talk with you about how humans have to prepare for the photon belt this time. What I'd like to know in detail is about what effect the photon belt has on the human body. To begin with, I understand that the Earth has already stepped into the territory of the photon belt. Is that right?

Yes, it is. The Earth has already stepped into the area of influence of the photon belt and it's in the entrance stage.

I see. How does the photon belt affect the human body?

To put the photon belt's function briefly, it changes the nature of material and makes it into the material of another dimension. Material becomes non-material and its nature also changes.

One of the reasons why an Earth human cannot live outside the atmosphere is because he has a physical body and it's not adapted to the Universe outside the atmosphere.

The most essential thing for human life is oxygen, and without it humans cannot survive. The photon belt aims to lift such human restriction, which means it changes the human DNA structure to create a structure which is adapted for space. In other words it changes the physical nature of the human body.

The change Earth humans can feel at the entrance of the photon belt is, they feel tired easily or the symptoms in their sick areas worsen. That is because their immune systems are put into chaos in order to adapt to the new environment. You get tired easily because your DNA begins to change by the photon belt and that's like a revolution to build a new nation. Revolution invariably accompanies pain, and there is also inner movement that tries to resist alien factors. As a result fierce tension arises and it tires your body even more.

What do you mean by inner movement that tries to resist alien factors?

It means inner movement that tries to resist new change. The photon belt also demands a shift in consciousness along with material's change of nature. Although the Universe is one gigantic mass, there is the distinction between the high and low sides. According to the level of dimension the high and low of the Universe is determined. The lower a dimension is, the lower the place it's located at and the higher the dimension is, the higher the place it is located at.

The Earth belongs to the 3rd dimension and due to the photon belt's influence it will jump to the 5th dimension. The photon belt aims to change the structure of materials which is of the 3rd dimension and to elevate it into the 5th dimension so that it can adapt itself there. The human consciousness should also be elevated to be able to stay in the 5th dimension.

Resistance to alien factors means the conflict between your body and mind; your body intends to change because of the influence of the photon belt, but your consciousness doesn't change in accordance. In other words your body and mind work separately. While your body wants to adapt itself to the new world showing the movement of change for dimension shift, your mind housed in your body is used to your old habit and so it cannot adapt itself well comparatively to the change for the dimension shift.

That is because your consciousness is still accustomed to materialistic thinking of the 3rd dimension. To get used to the 5th dimension that is the world of non-material, you have to free yourself from materialistic way of thinking. Since it's just the entrance stage of the photon belt, the influence your consciousness has on your body is minute. But when the photon belt exerts its influence to the fullest, your third dimensional consciousness which is accustomed to materialistic thinking will fail in passing through the photon belt and will bounce off. Therefore your body will die from intense pain.

Then do you mean whether one can pass through the photon belt or not depends on one's mind?

Yes. The photon belt is unseen energy and territory current Earthlings can't see. But this energy will change matter's trait and will eventually change the entire environment of the Earth. The condition to be able to survive in the new environment, is your mind.

Let me explain it with the concept of the empty heads of grain. Assume that the photon belt is water and the Earth is a vast vessel. If you pour water, the photon belt into a vessel, the Earth, the heavy fruits will sink down and empty and light ones will float on the surface of water.

A heavy fruit means you are preoccupied with a human way of thinking and your mind is full of greed and desire. A light fruit means your mind is emptied from them and so it's comparatively light.

In Earth humans' current state of mind that is full of competition, selfishness, greed, desire, possession, and attachment, it won't be easy for them to pass through the photon belt.

What phenomenon will happen if the human body cannot let photons pass through?

It can be compared to popcorn. If corn is current humans' state, the photon belt will change corn into non-material. It will change its form and traits to suit the 5th dimension. However, if corn cannot let the photons pass through, if it absorbs them and begins to bounce them, there will be an extreme change of energy inside. Its frequency will increase tremendously and it will pop in the end. The human body will fail to adapt.

It's terrible just to think of it, but that's the very fate humans have to face in the near future. That's a process for the dimension leap. If you prepare yourself well, you will be able to experience a completely new world with advanced consciousness under better circumstances. That will be a new kind of delight and excitement that the current humanity has never known.

Some people believe that the doom of the world will come in Dec. 2012, and the Mayan calendar says that the Earth's axis will stand erect. Experts who make astronomical observations feel the extraordinary movement in the Universe, and some groups are known to be preparing for forth coming disasters.

What is the condition to go through the influence of the photon belt safely and survive?

As I told you before the photon belt is necessary for dimension elevation. So you should follow the way of life in the world of the 5th dimension, not in the world of the 3rd dimension, the Earth. Some people are said to prepare shelters inside underground bunkers and reserve food for possible disasters, but the photon belt aims to penetrate material and change its nature or quality.

There is no place on the Earth that it cannot reach, so it's not easy to pass through it if you keep your old humanly habit. If they still have the current way of thinking, those places will turn into their tombs. That's also an ironic thing caused by materialism and ignorance about the Universe.

The condition to pass through the photon belt safely is a change in thinking, emotion and energy. Thinking is your thought; it must not be dominated by material. Admit the limitation of materialistic thinking and think thoughts which are one level higher. Rather than individualism based on self and family, you must have a community-centered thought of "we" as foundation to make your way through the present hardship.

The Consciousness of a Universe Citizen

I told you that the photon belt brings about matter's change in nature and quality. As your body is matter, the change of your mind that governs your body, is essential. If you cannot accommodate foreign factors different from you and don't have the mind of a universe citizen, your body ruled by your mind will not be able to withstand the photons.

The mind of a universe citizen means that we all are one. You and I are not two but one, and we are brothers and sisters that came from one root origin. In the core of that mind there is love. It doesn't mean narrow, family-centered love but means love in a broad sense to consider the Earth and the Universe as your family. Only when you have such an open mind, can photons safely pass through you.

In order to turn into the semi-ether body of the 5th dimension, a process to change old energy is necessary, and what's necessary in that process is universe energy, the energy of a high dimension. Universe energy accelerates the change of a cell's characteristics and it's also a very important element to enable a person get over the photon belt's influence more lightly. I can tell you that the most realistic preparation for the dimension shift caused by the photon belt is emptying your mind, having love and doing breathing training with universe energy.

You mean the most crucial thing is our consciousness. And having the consciousness of a universal citizen is the heart of the matter?

Exactly. You must know why the photon belt comes to the current humankind at this time point and what the Universe wants from humans through the Earth's revolution period. High dimension means high consciousness, and also means you are as close to the Universe as the level of your consciousness is. All this providence ultimately comes true by the will of the Universe. Humans must recognize the will of the Universe, put it into action and become one with it through the Earth's changing period.

I understand. Thank you for your good message.

The Community-oriented Life; the Eco-community

You said yesterday that we have to think a community-centered thought of "we" rather than "me" to pass through the photon belt. What does it specifically mean to think community-centered thoughts?

When you live in a community, you come to think community-oriented thoughts naturally. In fact, when cosmic beings visited the Earth in groups and transplanted their civilizations on the Earth, it didn't begin with one person and then grow to small groups as time passed. A certain number of people were transferred from the beginning; therefore we can say that they lived a community life from the beginning.

By the way, nowadays Earth people place too much value on their families. Their dedication and the amount of energy they put in their families are enormous. If it's too much, we call it family egoism. Won't it be difficult to steer away from this form of life with its long history, towards a community-oriented life?

As a family is the minimum unit which enables the successful propagation of a species, Earthlings are defensive about it and don't like others' intrusion. Now it's time for such consciousness to be broadened. As you graduate from elementary school and join middle school and high school, the time has come for Earth people's consciousness to grow to be mature.

Expand the scope of your family, and that will do. Make your neighbors your siblings, and Carol your next door neighbor will become one of your daughters.

That's a nice message, but I'm wondering if my mind and action will follow my understanding. Is there a good way to do it?

> If your thought changes, then your actions will change. To begin with if you think that you expand the scope of your family, that will do. And take even a very small action with that mindset.

To give it a careful thought, there seemed to have been much of community life in the modern history of humanity. So many countryside villages before industrialization were a typical community society. What do you think?

> Yes, they were. It was a community where culture and custom were respected under the same rules and tradition. Although there was an exclusive attitude about other cultures, it was a good role model for a community. They had educational institutes and rules to follow among members with the cultural foundation where they respected each other. However, as you are industrialized and urbanized, those kinds of communities no longer became valid.

Gandhi from India too was a philosopher and activist who thought much of a "village" and tried to change the world through community movement. What do you think of him?

> He was a cosmic being from another planet. He was such a great revolutionist, theologist and activist. Throughout his life he consistently held fast to his belief.

It looks like his thought of nonviolence and respect for life through village movement shows a good example of community life.

> His thought could have gone forward and spread as worldwide ideology or action, not restricted only

for Indians in his era. But unfortunately it was not adopted so much by Earth humans as a practical village movement. Even India went on the path of industrialization after independence from Britain.

What lesson can we learn from him?

It's insight ahead of his time. He already knew the harmful effect of material civilization. The reason such a poor country India could spread such spiritual movement and practice against Britain, a representative of material civilization was thanks to the one outstanding leader Gandhi, who was ahead of the times.

How does the Universe evaluate his Swaraj village movement?

With lifelong consistent thought and action, Gandhi intended to suggest how humans can reduce desires and live well, and to overcome inner violent nature. Ultimately the movement aimed to uplift human society to one level higher.

His great trait is, it's not easy for average thinkers to realize consistency in life between their thoughts and actions, but Gandhi put his ideas and thoughts into action thoroughly. He didn't just insist on peace, coexistence, self-governance and independence with words. Every moment, his action was the embodiment of his belief, and that's what was really great about him.

To live a community life, it seems that one of the parts which needs the highest degree of self-control is the desire for possession. Possessing people, possessing material and so on... In this respect Gandhi's village seems to be a really advanced model.

He led people so well to control their intrinsic desires. As India was under the colonial rule of Britain, his movement became a pivot and generated power which brought people together.

I think he was such a great man, indeed. It seems many great people in the history of humanity thought of community life or utopia life beyond the scope of family. Were they pre-assigned a certain role when they were born on the Earth?

Yes, many people came from the Universe with missions to lead humankind to evolution. Gandhi and Plato were amongst them, and among those who led worldwide communities there were some people who received the waves from the Universe. That's universe planets' involvement for the sake of the Earth's evolution.

Who is Thoreau, the author of "Walden"? He built a cabin on the lakeshore of Walden and lived alone. He showed people how nice simple life in nature outside material civilization is, and his book inspired many people including Gandhi. Was he also from another planet in the Universe?

As a sensitive and bright poet and writer, he received the wave of the Universe. He was an ecologist in modern terms. A lot of people at the time and in later ages longed for his beautiful and calm life at his cabin. He showed them the fact that life doesn't need so many things, and inspired a lot of intellectuals and thinkers. In such serenity you can receive the wave of the Universe easily.

In the U.S., communities by Hippies were naturally formed in 1960's, which initiated and spread community life. I used to envy Hippies freedom... What do you think of Hippies?

The movement in response to material civilization in the U.S. was Hippie culture. They knew the harmful effects of the vast organization, nation and material civilization and rejected them. It was a natural phenomenon.

When material civilization reaches a certain level, reaction against it arises and people get to explore different ways of life. Hippie culture was an American style of alternative culture against material civilization. There were some people that were ahead of the time and there were others that just couldn't adapt themselves to society. Nevertheless it's obvious that they lived a community existence together.

That way humankind has continued in community life uninterrupted.

Yes. Nothing can develop overnight like magic. History goes on while someone challenges a new task, complements and corrects the result in trials and errors. Now humankind has reached a stage where they try to put together various kinds of trials and embody a new way of life.

Part 5

Chapter 12

The Cosmic Beings Who were once on the Earth

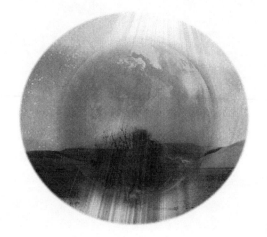

Socrates

Marlin, today, I'd like to talk about Socrates, one of the figures from history. What does he currently do on his planet?

He is not currently staying on his planet. After having completed his mission at that time, he is now in the higher dimension in the Universe.

Ah, then you mean he is an enlightened being now?

Yes, that's right. He is a role model to us cosmic beings. His achievement on the Earth was highly valued because he had completed his mission successfully, and he was promoted to a much higher level at that time. He is one of the enviable figures whom we respect very much.

Before he came to the Earth, what did he do on his planet?

Well... I think it would be better if you met Socrates in person and ask him. Since I contacted him in advance, he is waiting now.

(After regulating my breaths for a while, I call Socrates.)

Mr. Socrates, my name is Roar from the planet Earth. Though I am not good enough to talk to you, may I ask for your teaching?

Hello, nice to meet you. I'm Socrates. I have been waiting for this conversation which was scheduled for today

-All right. I intended to talk with you with a bit of a comfortable mind thinking you were on your home planet, but after I heard that you're an enlightened being now, I feel a little burdened all of a sudden.

Please ease yourself. This conversation is very essential at this time, and I hope you will converse with me in comfort.

Thank you. I feel very embarrassed to hear such kind words from you who is at such a high stage I cannot possibly think that I will understand well.

Ha ha ha! Our conversation is a formal one, not just a small talk between you and me. It's the process to deliver my will to humans. So I respect you as a public figure. How about going on with our conversation in an interview format? I think it will be better if we tell stories while you become a reporter and I become an interview.

Ok, I understand. I think it'll also ease my mental burden if I become a reporter and ask questions of you. All right, let me start.

What did you do on your planet before you came to the Earth?

Before I came to the Earth, I was dealing with military affairs.

Do the military affairs refer to strategies and tactics used in wars?

Yes.

I think it doesn't match the life path which you followed on the Earth.

One of the methods that can edify a soul, is through a war. It is rather shocking, but through wars you can study tremendous things in a short time. A war is one of the methods to control the evil in order to proceed along your way towards the Universe. Numerous pains and sorrows are latent in it, but in order to balance the world, a war is taken as a tool.

Here, evil can imply many things. There are evils committed by those with vested interests for their greed and desires, whereas stagnation due to too much comfort and indolence also brings about evils. War can be used as a shock tactic to awaken souls. Just like when energy in the human body becomes stagnant, it can cause serious diseases including cancers, when the consciousness of humanity becomes stagnant and cancerous, a war is necessary to control it.

Oh, really? Nowadays I am realizing the meaning of the words that in the midst of pains a person can grow. By the way, why did you not choose military affairs when you came to Earth from your planet?

I wanted to try a method of edifying people in a more peaceful manner. In the aspect of edification, I noticed that the methods were different but the influence on people's souls was just the same; this is why I made that decision when I was born on the Earth.

While I was researching data, I found a record that your appearance was ugly. Is that true?

Hahaha! If you saw my face at that time, you might say 'he turns me off' or something like that. But I chose such an appearance on purpose. It was true that I was a little ugly but you should rather say, I was 'not good looking'. I think that would be a better description. I chose that appearance because I did not want the original meaning of my words to be mistaken, because humans are deceived by appearances and misinterpret things. In order to raise the objectivity of my words it was necessary that I didn't show myself as attractive. So, I chose an appearance that was not good-looking, not ugly though.

Ah, there is such a profound hidden meaning. If you see contemporary people, you'll know that "Lookism" is rampant in our society. It's true that the person physical looks are looks pretty or handsome is given a higher status in modern society. So, plastic surgery has been booming and everyone has been overly interested in their appearance.

Correct. Because of that reason, I chose that path as a method to pass on truth considering humans' characteristic at that time.

It's said that you got married and had a wife and three sons, is that right?

Yes, that's right.

It's said that your household was poor then, how come?

I maintained the same household as ordinary people. I was satisfied with the lifestyle to the degree that

I didn't have problems in my living. I didn't want more or less than that. Using present terms, I had a simple life. For a person like a philosopher, if you live in excess, it won't be helpful for you to study philosophy, so I blocked it beforehand.

It's said that you were an eloquent speaker. You used your unique questioning method when you conversed with sophists. And, using that method, you made the sophists look at their opinion objectively and eventually confess that they didn't know anything. Your descendants are using the method as an educational tool called Socratic "elenchus", or the Socratic Questioning Method. Would you introduce that method to us?

Sure, I will.

My method was to allow a person to present his opinion as much as he wants to tell. You listen to his opinion from his perspective completely. Then I ask him to explain some specific parts. I listen to his logic about why he thinks he is right once again. Then I liken their logic to something that is similar but results in an entirely different answer. And I let the person compare the two cases. In other words, from the structure of those set up logics $1+1+1+1+1$ equals 5, but I give him another example that can be wrong. In that way, I help the person to realize for himself that his idea is not entirely correct.

The core of my method was to destroy the structure of logic. The beliefs that people have are built up based on experiences they have previously had. Therefore, they measure the world with their own standard. I led conversation so that they could realize that the standard could be applied differently according to circumstances and what they had experienced was not entirely right but only partially right. The intention of my questioning method was to let them form a viewpoint and ask questions that could include the whole, not a part; its essence begins from the point "I know nothing." When they realized what they had thought was right was not right, what they thought they knew, they didn't actually know, they became fairly confused. For the intellectual, it needed significant courage to acknowledge that they were ignorant, and it hurt their pride. So, I had many enemies at that time.

You said 'Know Thyself', which is one of the famous sayings you left. What was the meaning of those words?

Know Thyself… (He looks up the sky for a while and casts his mind.)

People of my time were so far removed from original human beings. Though it's the same today, in the old era, when the internet or info-communications had not been developed, people had no option but to build up their philosophy of life based on just what they could see or hear; that was the reality of those days. Not only the governing class but also the public people were blinded by their own greed and lured by the profits right in front of them and they committed unjust deeds without hesitation if those seemed to bring benefits to them. The public upheld those who brought them profits while the ruling class noticed such mind frames of the citizens and publicly made up the philosophy to justify those doings to take advantage of such minds in clever ways. I had to say something that could awaken them, so I said, "Know yourself." I said this in the hope that they could realize their real selves and discover their original natures and live according to it.

What is the real self of a human being?

The real self of a human being is One. To describe it in a word, it is the original nature. The real self of a human being refers to this, and it signifies the mind of the Creator who created the Universe. All of us are creatures born with the love of the Creator as well as the beings to contribute to the evolution of the Universe by assisting the Creator.

How did the citizens respond to your words, "Know thyself!"?

Their responses were really varied. Some people questioned their real existence, and many people were given a chance to think about their actions through contemplating those words. They were very useful words to let them stop for a while and reflect on themselves by examining their actions. Of course, the depth of their reflection would differ from person to person, but it was effective to let them stop on their way of life and think.

You were charged with corrupting the minds of youths and being unfaithful to Athenian gods by Greek citizens and finally sentenced to death. Many of your disciples tried to persuade you to escape from prison to save you, but you chose to stay. Instead, you said, "A law is a law, however undesirable it may be." And that makes modern people remember you as a glorious saint. What is the reason that you didn't escape even if you could have? Why did you accept the contradictory situation of that time, while saying "A law is a law, however undesirable it may be".

It was to complete my philosophy. It was in order to make my words and logic real that I told people to stay alive in their hearts, I needed a firm faith in the truth, so

I accepted death. If I had run away in order to continue to live while giving up my belief as a philosopher at that time, my philosophy would be nothing but the excuse of a coward. Through my final death study, I was able to complete my faith in the Universe.

The words, 'A law is a law, however undesirable it may be" imply that I will accept my destiny. Because I was supposed to die, I followed my destiny and obeyed the calling from the Universe. Death brings huge lessons to humans. My death brought about many controversies to the people of those days, and provided a chance with sophists, who just kept glibness to reflect on the dreadful power of speeches.

You were not afraid to die then?

I was not afraid of death as I knew who I was. 'Knowing' is that important. You can get liberated from ignorance when you know. The condition to know is to deny yourself; that is no-selfness. You should keep maintaining a mindset that you do not know anything. That's the truth, and the beginning of knowing.

Thank you for your precious words. Would you leave a last message for the people of today?

Fundamentally, people should start their lives from knowing oneself. You cannot say you are the host of your life if you do not know who you are. If you live just the life given to you as it is without being aware of where you came from and where you are heading to, how fruitful and valuable can it be? The true value of yourself doesn't lie in money, fame or love. Self-introspection is far more valuable. In this respect, let me give you my last message: "Know Thyself!"

Thank you for your very precious teachings. I was
delighted and happy throughout the conversation.
I give my deep gratitude to you Socrates that you
allowed me to have this conversation with you.

Scott and Helen Nearing

I'd like to have a special meeting today, could you help me?

Who would you like to meet?

Scott and Helen Nearing! Can I meet them?

Sure. I've contacted them beforehand. I've known that
you wanted to see them.

Let me introduce them to you. Here they are.

Hi, Scott and Helen.

Hello, I'm Scott. I am called Morae on my planet.

Here comes Helen. Helen, please greet him.

Hi, I'm Helen Nearing.

It's my double honor to meet both of you together. I'm so
glad to meet you.

Helen, what do you do on the planet?

H: I work on healing people's minds and the growth
of nature and plants.

My name is Se-na-yah.

Se-na-yah!! Is that right?

Yes, that's right.

You're working with nature there, too. I can feel that your
energy is soft and natural.

S: My work is architecture and engineering. Our lives
on the Earth together were happy and we were able

to complete our callings together. I feel so grateful for Helen. Without her, I would not have spent the evening of my life so naturally and happily like that. She supported me in many ways.

What do you think, Helen? Were you also happy with your life with Scott? What did you like about him especially? Though it's a little embarrassing to ask directly like this... I was just wondering about it.

H: I liked Scott's strong spiritual power and executive ability when he made up his mind that something's right. He had no fear, unlike ordinary intellectuals. I admired his living according to his philosophy with courage and willpower; and the reflection about what he thought in his life.

This question could also be embarrassing but I wonder... Helen, you were in your 20s, and you fell in love with Scott, a divorced man, who was 20 years older than you. I think you were a little blinded by love... Helen, what were you thinking when you married your father's friend?

H: I had already been disappointed by worldly or human love. When I met Scott, I felt he was a nice person and that he was a fellow traveler as a spiritual colleague, a life partner and was a person I could respect. Our love was not the color of thick pink but the thin green of spring or the sky blue. I was rarely disappointed by him while I was with him because we could understand each other deeply and each one's pursuit in life was so similar.

I can feel and see. I thought life could be this beautiful after reading your book. Scott, excuse me. Let me talk a little more talk with Helen.

S: No problem, I'm all right. I'm enjoying just listening to your talk. I feel flattered to hear you praising me.

Helen, you went out with Krishnamurti at one time. What did you get from the relationship with him? Scott, please understand me, even if you feel a little bad, you know, a love story is the common topic of all ages.

H: Krishnamurti was famous as an ascetic from an early age. At that time, I wanted to pursue a spiritual path with him as his love and disciple. But after some time I was a little disappointed with him. Because I realized that his words and actions did not coincide and I was used by him. Truth is more important than anything in a human relationship but I felt our relationship was not based on that. I made up my mind to end our relationship first. Although this would become wide spread throughout the world, I felt the relationship was not right.

Ah, I understand. I can feel your courage... Scott, I think you couldn't be happier when you met an attractive young lady like Helen. What was it you liked about Helen?

S: Helen was a pure and quiet person like a deep well. She and I made an appointment to meet each other on the Earth. Our role was to show a model life to people on the Earth. Without Helen, that would have been so hard. She changed me into a flexible man from a harsh one. Our life was a kind of model but it was not artificial like posing as a model. We were just content with our lives.

You don't know how hard it is to meet such a fantastic partner like you did? I think you were given a good chance when you came to Earth, I envy you. I'd like to give you an "Award of Best Couple on the Earth".
You had a life of self-sufficiency, were vegans and made things you needed or bartered. You lived a life where you had few needs or reasons to earn money... I think actually

you were the first line of blacklist entrepreneurs or those whom stock-keepers hated most... How did you actually feel by living such a way of life?

S: I became more convinced that my theory and faith were right. I think people can doubt if such a life is really happy. But from that life, we realized that there is nothing much that human beings need and also, where true harmony came from. How did you feel, Helen?

H: I also had utmost happiness. The first thing we earned was peace of mind. Also if you do some physical work, you will maintain your health, and if you produce something, it will make your life rich and abundant. The reason those who only consume cannot be healthy is because they don't have the joy of producing something. Your life close to the Earth gives you stability and understanding about the reasons of nature. Our life on the Earth was the time when our minds were sound while spirits became profound. I think we had the best experience we could have had on the Earth.

Helen, did you know your mission during your life on the Earth?

H: First I just thought I was living my own life but then I realized that I should share our lifestyle and ideas with many people on the Earth. I came to know that I could deliver our lifestyle more effectively through writing books after showing a model, rather than traveling a lot and telling our story. If we had always been busy going around and getting along with people, we would have ended our lives as just theorists or preachers.

I agree. It has left bigger effects on modern people all over the world for you to have written books after showing a life model.

Scott, according to 'Comprehensive Plan for Mankind', you asserted that: 1. Nature as a common property of mankind must be preserved and used well, 2. Planned community must be established on the Earth, 3. The greatest health and happiness for the greatest number of people must be guaranteed by a proficient world government ...
As for human's way of life, you had faith in eco-community but you didn't try it, I am wondering what the reason was.

> S: While I was living with Helen, I suggested a community life to people around us many times. However, they were so afraid of a new way of life because of their thoughts and faiths. I could not force them to lead such a life. However, I felt it firmly that it was an ideal model for humanity and people on the Earth should live together that way someday.

There were many communities in USA at that time; didn't you think you should join them?

> H: Yes, I thought about that. There were many hippie communities in the 60s as well as established religious communities. However, the community I wanted to build was not a hippie-like community. They were too sexually promiscuous and emphasized only freedom rather than accountability. I did not agree with that. I wanted a religious community even less. Therefore, I tried to build a new community, but it wasn't realized.

I think your mission was likely to be showing humanity an example of a harmonious life with nature and human growth, escaping from the harm of materialism, not building a community and showing the life within it. What was the extent of your mission?

> H: You're right. Our mission was not to build a community to show everything, but rather showing people's heart a model where humans can live

beautifully and harmoniously with nature. Our mission was to give a chance and motive to think of how harmonious a human's life can be, what color the love between humans can be, or what the purpose of life should be.

Ah, I see. Scott, would you tell me about the organized community you think is ideal?

S: It's a society where humans are respected. Or it's a life-style where humans are not controlled by materials and can obtain food, clothes and a place to sleep from working with nature. It's a simple life-style where a human's spirit grows and can share something with others even a little bit. More than anything else, people should stop killing each other, destroying each other or breaking into war. If you harm others, it is the same as harming yourself. When you become aware of this, society can grow together. Humans should try to study diligently to awaken such consciousness.

I can feel the same energy here that I felt in your book "Conscience of a Radical". You mentioned world government. How is community life related to world government?

S: When people shift to community life and many communities are built, I think it's desirable that they don't belong to a certain nation, and the world government manages the communities and preserves happiness, health and security of people. It doesn't refer to a dictatorial government.

It works as an international organization and makes its decisions on important matters such as a blueprint for the Earth's humankind. The people who are flexible, elastic and wise will comprise that organization and humankind will live an entirely different life.

That's what I expected from you Scott. Does it not make the president feel threatened? (I laugh)
Helen, your dinner table is very simple and really beautiful. Maybe, I think it's the lightest meal ever amongst Americans.

H: We enjoyed unprocessed natural simple food. We didn't cook complicated meals, we enjoyed food in its raw state not containing fragrant spices or additives at all. We mostly ate the fruits and vegetable in season. Also we pickled or bottled them lightly and could eat the stored food after the season. This food makes your spirit pure and healthy, and also makes your body light also. Thus we almost never had to see a doctor.

You filled your dinner table with natural foods, was it not a little boring to eat them every day?

H: No. If you eat less and exercise properly, your mind and spirit become purified, and greed or avarice for something disappears. Your desire for food is very harmful for your health. If you desire delicacies that means your heart feels hollow or you're unsatisfied with something emotionally. If your life is not that, your desire for food is also controlled naturally and you can become moderate.

Would you teach me one of your recipes you were good at?

H: I wasn't a good cook. I didn't cook food based on certain recipes or existing ideas, which means I didn't think there is a fixed method to deal with food. I just made a simple recipe that came across my mind every day and had it joyously.

I enjoyed making salads. Every ingredient is possible. I cut vegetables and fruits in season and added one or two sauces or natural dressings I had stored, and ate them right away. Then I felt their fresh and brisk energy filling my whole body.

I'd like to hear Scott's opinion on vegetarian diet. What' the reason you refrained from eating meat?

S: Both humans and animals are living creatures. Is there a particular reason why you eat meat? I don't think it is reasonable to kill something in order to eat. Animals have the right to be protected because they are alive. It doesn't seem right to raise livestock in order to eat them. I wanted to let people know that they could have a richer life without eating meat. You know how much energy is taken in raising stock. Eating meat originated from human covetousness.

I am also living on a mostly vegetarian diet. Furthermore, foot and mouth disease has run rampant and the entire country of South Korea is unsettled because of that.

S: Right, humanity's greed has caused it. I think you'd better promote a vegetarian diet more strongly at this time. Living a good life with animals is also the work humans have to do in these days.

Scott, you were said to be a wonderful speaker… it is that true?

S: I wasn't a wonderful speaker, but I just led the lecture with my sincerity and passion. My intention to change the world as a reformer was transmitted to the audience. Truth has power and people had a longing for the new world in their hearts.

Now I would like to change topics, and I'd like to talk about your death.

You stopped eating when you turned 100 years old, and stepped toward your death while Helen was watching you. Weren't you afraid to die?

S: When my body got weaker and my consciousness became confused, I knew it was time for me to complete my life. It was the moment when I put into action what I had been thinking about; how one's completion of life should be. I wanted to wrap up my life well by doing that rather than being afraid. I felt that was a natural process. Besides, Helen was with me and watching my last days on the earth, so I wasn't so lonely or in pain. I thought life and death would just be circulating as the law of nature did.

Helen, what did you feel while letting your longtime partner Scott leave and watched him face his death?

H: I anticipated hollowness and I felt his empty seat for long after he left. But I thought that death is a natural process. I also thought of death all the time and I regarded it as a process to prepare for another life while ending the previous one.

I was moved by your life-long journey as a couple and its completion was so beautiful. Helen, after you let your beloved Scott leave, how was your life, living alone?

H: I reflected on our life and I wrote a book... My everyday life still continued. It was not different from before. Recalling the times we spent together and the publication of books were another joy for me.

Now, it is time to complete our talk. Helen, what was your most precious learning in that life on the Earth?

H: My learning from a life on the Earth was evolving in harmony. My experience of expulsion when I was young, made me grow faster. It helped me to learn that I should not expect too much about humans and love. We lived up to our philosophy. We didn't spare our efforts and devotion in order to make harmony between nature, the two of us, and the people around us.

If I were asked what life is, I would say life is the delight of making an effort as well as the joy of putting something into action. My life as Helen on the Earth was happy and meaningful. Also I thank Scott very much.

Scott, thank you so much.

I really enjoyed my life with you, my husband and spiritual colleague.

S: (Scott seems to smile.)
Scott, you had already predicted community life as the future of humankind.
I think now is the time that we cannot delay having such a life any longer.
Would you give us your last message?

S: Life is beautiful. The present humankind has an extraordinary chance. Harmony is a process of striving for evolution. You need to make efforts for that. In order to have the good life, you need to make an effort and love each other and strive for that. Helen and I tried to show what that is on the Earth. It is your turn now. Do not spare any effort to achieve harmony and love.

Helen and Scott, thank you.
I was happy to meet you.

We were too... Thank you.

A Saint of the Jungle - Albert Schweitzer

I would like to know about Dr. Albert Schweitzer. He lived as a doctor and theologian in Africa. I would like to know about him as he is called a "saint of the jungle" for having worked for many people through his missionary work and medicine.

Let me see. Does he have anything to do with love?

In the future, we will have to go without convenient communication systems. So I want to find out how to convey love in other ways. Some figures who have lived such a life came into my mind. Through the conversation with Dr. Schweitzer, I would like to learn about how to deliver love to others.
Ah... Doctor. Where are you now? Where has he gone all of a sudden...?

> Don't mind him. I asked him for consent because I would like to speak with you directly.

Oh... I see. Doctor, where do you stay now?

> I have been staying in Pleiades. Now I am here on the Earth.

What? Do you mean that you are living here now, meaning that you are here on the Earth?

> Yes, I do. Though it is hard to believe, I have such an ability.

Do you have two selves then? Another self of yours? How is it possible??

> It would be difficult to explain about that in detail. Let's have our talk.

I see. At any rate, I am glad to see you. I saw a movie about you before. I was impressed at your playing the piano in the jungle. How did you become so good at music?

> I had much free time. Geniuses like me would master anything quite soon after starting it. I also enjoyed music because my wife was fascinated by my piano playing.

Well...

> ...What?

You must be Marlin?

Ah, ha ha ha! I am caught. I talked to you in disguise of the doctor for dramatic fun. Don't get angry about that. Was it interesting anyway?

Ah, I see! But please tell me about him.

Dr. Albert Schweitzer is in activity on the Earth now. Though he is not a medical man, he is fully active somewhere on the Earth.

He was a man who knew about the Universe and who loved human beings. He started as a theologian. One day when he served as a professor of theology, he had the mind to put his theology into practice without just studying and lecturing it. He wanted to put love into practice and realize love, the core of the Bible, on the Earth.

Therefore, he got onto a ship bound for Africa. Of course, he went there with several family members, but it was not an ordinary situation. Schweitzer a professor of theology obtained a license for medicine after being taught by professors who were previously his colleagues, and then moved to Africa. His wife became a nurse to work with him; this is all about what a wonderful couple can be; a husband and a wife who helped each other. Don't you envy them?

Sometimes yes, sometimes no.

Dr. Albert Schweitzer left for Africa with his family. While he studied theology, he was called a liberal theologian. He was open to various thoughts and viewpoints and had much reverence for life. He loved not only human beings but also all living things.

He played the pipe organ and studied theology, but he had always kept one thought in mind that he would like to make others feel the happiness which filled him. He had wanted to spread his happiness around. When he was child, he sometimes got up at night without his mother's knowledge and chanted the Lord's Prayer for insects and animals to demonstrate his reverence for life. When he was over thirty years old, he could not stand the fact that he alone was so happy. So he made up his mind to do missionary work. It was his most fundamental insight and wish that all living creatures would be happy.

I see. You know him well. What do you think of him from the viewpoint of the Universe? He had caused many new movements to happen on the Earth. There have been many followers. Many people like the "Doctors Without Borders" take care of life with their love and medicine. He was also well-known for working against nuclear experiments and weapons, along with Dr. Einstein. He won a Nobel Prize for peace and became famous all over the world. Is he famous in the Universe too?

Yes, he is. He is famous. The planet Earth itself is famous. The Earth emitted powerful energy in the vortex of wars, huge energies. But it was not always so pure.

Purifying and making use of the energy of the Earth, the Universe had watched the Earth. As he started his activity, the energy changed little by little. The power of the energy – love – to overcome his practical difficulties was strong and suggested a way forward for many cosmic beings who had observed the Earth.

Life in the Universe could not be more peaceful. Cosmic beings live long and there are not various kinds of energy. Therefore, love is a natural flow so that we call it circulation rather than the name "love".

But his love in the situation of war was spreading itself, overcoming all the barriers in reality. The energy of his love was getting stronger and stronger so that the energy gradually began to permeate into the consciousness of people. Those who were moved by that had the same thought as his one by one. His love for all the living creatures, the seed that he cherished in his heart, began to be widely spread all around. The sight was as beautiful as the birth of a new planet.

I understand. According to a book that deals with his life in Africa, he regarded the natives not as equal but as inferior beings and the book evaluated him as a devil of the jungle rather than a saint of the jungle. What was the truth?

It may be correct to call him an eccentric of the jungle. The medical skills of the doctor who showed abilities like that of an "otunga", a magician in local African language, made the Africans think of him as a god. The patients who were deadly sick took medicines and suddenly got well. Legs where the pus oozed out got better in a few days. All such things were mysterious to the eyes of the native people.

They became attached only to the visible phenomena because they didn't understand the medical principles and the doctor's intention. He was just a person who cured them. The hospital was just a place where they could find something to eat. Therefore, they didn't usually stick to what he told them in order to keep their diseases from recurring. He treated the patients and gave medicine to them, but they often returned with aggravated conditions the next day. Here he encountered a humane despair.

He didn't care what people around him said. "I don't care even if they tell me, a theologian not to talk about the Bible, I don't care that people call me an idiot who gave up a comfortable life in Europe. As far as I can share the love in myself with others, that is enough." He had this idea, but he became frustrated and despaired when those who had received treatment and love from him, didn't understand and thank him and sometimes even shunned him. Fortunately his despair didn't last long. He had his wife with him, who always reminded him of why they had come there. He could keep going on without losing his direction.

Some say that he had some notion of white supremacy because he said, "You and I are brothers, but I am your older brother."

Of course, he had. But he only said that as a manner of speech. What should a mother say if she saw her child pick up something from the ground and eat it?

Sometimes strict education is necessary. It is necessary to strictly teach that wrong things are wrong. It might be nice to make everything understood in logic, but it is impossible to persuade everyone with logic. Instead of trying to do so, it was a much faster way to find more people who would follow him. The natives, who at first didn't follow him, but watched what he was doing, finally opened their minds and accepted him. The piano which he brought to Africa with him played a great role in opening the hearts of the natives.

Do you remember the scene of Gabriel playing the oboe in the movie *The Mission*? It is often a more accessible way to communicate with the natives when verbal communication is blocked. So it is necessary to appeal to their feelings with a beauty that everyone can feel. You and I began to converse through feelings in this way, didn't we? Turn the feelings into words and into images. The communications between the people on the Earth are the same.

Human beings do not listen with their ears. What one hears through the ears is very distorted by the existing system of thinking; however a message passed on in the form of feeling, directly touches the listener's soul beyond speech. You don't hear your sweetheart's words as just speech, do you? It is the same. All the senses a person has can be activated to grasp the true meaning of the other party. To do that, it is most essential to open the person's heart. This is why culture is so important. Music can sometimes accurately deliver more things than language.

I see. He made a great contribution in changing conscious-ness through missionary work with medicine and making and spreading new notions of service and love for human-ity. I am surprised that one person could do all those things.

It is not difficult. Anyone could do it if they think it is possible. The principle is simple. The feeling of love is basically set in the mind of human beings. So the most important thing is how to touch the love. Have you ever fallen in love? Then you will find it the same in winning another's heart.

I think I must be full of light first to win another's heart.

You're right. But please don't make it too difficult. If you begin to practice little things right now, the light will spread little by little. So it is more important than anything else to deliver your warm heart. It can even be just a bowl of soup that is a bowl of love.

I appreciate your good advice. From the viewpoint of a cosmic being what do you think is the greatest achievement Dr. Schweitzer made?

It is that he made the concept of love for all humanity and had many descendants of that notion. I have never lived on the Earth. However, watching the situations on the Earth I cannot understand, I have wondered what was happening there. As soon as they are born, people live as if wearing a one ton sandbag; increasing the weight of the barbells endlessly at the gym. Human beings have always lived like that, not just now, but since they appeared on the Earth for the first time. The heaviest burden is emotion. From the viewpoint of cosmic beings who have few ups and downs of emotion, the passionate lives of the people there are just like morning soap operas on TV that people speak ill of, but get endlessly addicted to. Nevertheless, the message that is carried through them is clear. The life of each person itself is a human drama to us and we are touched by it. Cosmic beings are sometimes touched to tears by the people on the Earth who live with such heavy emotions. The descendants of Dr. Schweitzer exist everywhere. People say that a Dr. Schweitzer appears in every place. You know the Korean Schweitzer Dr. Kiryeo Jang and the Catholic priest Taeseok Lee, the hero of the documentary *Don't Cry Tons*. His descendants like them, who inherited the idea that one should work for humanity, are the very Schweitzers who are working on the Earth.

I see. Do you mean Dr. Schweitzer doesn't stay on the Earth?

Yes I do. You will know some day. But until then, please, think about what your life will be like at the time of the Earth's great change, with reference to his life. Your life will be like that of his in the future.

It's heartbreaking to think about that. He lived in a situation similar to ours.

> You're right. That is why you received the wave that guided you to study the life of Dr. Schweitzer carefully. Life on the Earth is a series of hardships. Then by whom were such hardships set up? It is you the human beings who set your lives up in such ways before you were born. It is just like abusing your body at the gym. It is just like studying at a university overnight. Don't you enjoy having lessons? Then, please remember that your present situation is a puzzle of your own making. Then you may accept the situation not as a difficulty but as a game.

Thank you. Marlin, you have never been born on the Earth. How do you know all this so well?

> There is nothing I don't know. You may think of me as a library. I am the very being who has been accumulating the databases of infinite information, all the data of the Universe. There are still many more stories to be told. I can tell you such stories not just for one thousand days but for one hundred billion years. For stories more than the number of stars and planets are being made in the Universe even now.

Mother Teresa, Mother of the Poor

Marlin, I would like to converse with Mother Teresa today. Before I get to talk to her, I have some questions to ask about her . Is this ok with you?

> Yes, of course. What would you like to know?

What does Mother Teresa do now on her home planet?

> Her specialty is love. She is taking care of a garden on her planet now. She has been just back from the

Earth so she is kind of having a rest while taking care of the garden. This is the same as mothers who have postnatal rest on the Earth.

How is her life on Earth evaluated?

It is considered successful because she played her role faithfully. It is successful because she gave the message that should be sent to the Earth people clearly. She planned to give people unconditional love. She loved Heaven with her whole mind and soul while staying in the lowest level of society. Her devotional love played a great role in purifying the minds of Earth people.

Hello, Mother Teresa. It is a great honor to see you.

I am glad to see you too.

As I begin to speak , I feel the energy of love filling my heart.

(She smiles.) That is my compassion for human beings. I loved them wholly and passionately with such a heart.

Wow, that's such a great love. It feels closer to the feeling of passion rather than of love. Is this really your love, Mother Teresa? It is really burning.

I wanted to love wholeheartedly; with my whole body and mind. I wanted to love God who also resided in the people of low places. As I had such a mindset, my heart could overflow with burning love which was not dampened. The love was the driving force which enabled me to get over any suffering and difficult situations.

It is impossible to do service called sacrifice without having such a mind. Without a burning love in the heart, the hardships and difficulties that come from the bottom of life feel limitlessly bigger and bigger. I could love people wholly despite all the hardships, thanks to the image of God I met in them. Through my attitude to serve them with all my mind and body as if they were God, they could also find the figure of God in me. To do such work was happier and more pleasant than anything else.

Ah, I have had the same intense love when I met my first love. My heart leaped and bounced. I have never had such a powerful love since then, but I'm feeling it in my heart right now. Not for anything or anyone. Ah, I am so deeply touched. Is this true passionate love?

> Yes, it is. It is an excitement. Love is heart-throbbing. It is love that makes your heart leap so hard that you wouldn't be able to sleep from the excitement. Such love makes you really forget about yourself and you fall into a mindless state, a No Mind state. This is how I loved people. I felt my heart throbbed every day to meet God who comes down in the poor. I was happiest when I got so excited from that feeling. That was the driving force of my unlimited energy.

I think I could go to the remotest corner of the Earth if I have love like this. Now I can understand the meaning of love a bit more.

> There is a saying that people filled with love can never stay still when they witness the pain of others. That means the same. People with powerful love flowing in their heart know what to do. Therefore, they cannot help but be voluntary workers. Love gets bigger and bigger if it is shared. The sense of being fulfilled obtained from it is too great to describe.

I would like to love. I also want to love passionately.
I would like to know and love the Universe that resides in
the wholly low positions.

What are you waiting for? Go out there, and you
will find beings to love everywhere. Share your
love with them. Your love will grow bigger and
bigger as you share it. You will experience the love
of the Universe wholly in your growing love. Just
love others.

I understand. I will love, share it with others and understand greater love.

Love is not something great. Love arises from a
little concern. You will experience a bigger love in
the course of putting a little concern into practice.
Love doesn't get close to you under some great
and wonderful name. Realize love through your
neighbors. You will find love while you are sharing.

Thank you, Mother Teresa. I feel that the name Mother
matches you well. Now you have taken off your physical
body what should I call you? You were called Mother but it
was while you were on the Earth.

My name is Marine in my home planet. Call me
Marine. You may call me by a name easy to deliver to
others.

I see. Marine. That is a very big and pretty name.

Thank you.

Thank you. I feel some at ease when you talk. That is really
good.

Now I feel like I have just returned alive from a battle
field and this is a leisurely mind that one who returned
can have while looking back to a life on the Earth.

I see. Why did you choose to live as a nun on the Earth?

That role was required on the Earth, so I applied for it. That role was necessary in order to show the love of the Universe which resides in low places. When people served Heaven, the churches at that time only worshiped and revered Heaven which only existed in the sky. Thus, they stayed in the churches and made efforts to find God there. For those people, the Earth required a model that actually shows one's belief through action. You know a person who serves God that resides at low places. It was necessary to broaden the limited viewpoints of Christians. Their spirituality had stagnated. It was necessary to broaden the width of their thinking in order to smooth their stagnated flow in growing spirituality. So as a means to do so, I wanted them to see the precious love of the Universe which resides in the poor people. Because the Universe intended to make them understand that it loves people irrespective of rank; I played the role.

You did your missionary work in India. Did you have any special reason for that?

At that time, the largest number of poor people lived there. In India, many people are branded as Untouchable by the cast system, live poor and painful lives and then hand the poverty and sufferings down from generation to generation. People may be divided into the poor and the rich on the principles of capitalism. Yet, the unequal social structure which designates people as noble or untouchable from birth is the lowest place made by human beings. India was the proper place for me to play my role at that time.

I understand.

Marine, you said you felt you had another vivid calling over and above your life's calling when you prayed quietly on a train from Calcutta to Darjeeling on the way to your annual retreat. You made up your mind to leave the convent and dedicate yourself to helping the poor while living among them. You called this day the "Day of Inspiration". Would you please tell me what message you received on the train from Calcutta to Darjeeling?

On the train, I was doing a lot of thinking, looking at the scenes outside. Watching beggars and children begging especially, I thought about myself who prayed for God's grace in my quiet life of prayer like a frog in a well. And I prayed for them earnestly. I prayed sincerely that God's love might be delivered to them and that they might be saved by the hands of God. At the moment, a clear voice was heard.

"My dear daughter! I am in pain. I need your helping hand. I want you to deliver the love which I cannot deliver to them. You will be able to meet me at the end of the way on which you walk." That was a very clear voice. At the moment all my body trembled and I shed endless tears at God's love and I made up my mind. I would receive the intention wholly which the universe gave me and put it into practice all my life.

Ah, you did so. What a touching story!

Your letters to Father Picachy were published into a book against your will, which shows that you had gone through many tests and trials of your dedicated love. You expressed your grave doubts about God's existence and pain over your lack of faith: "God does not want me." "Where is my faith? Even deep down ... there is nothing but emptiness and darkness ... If there be God, please forgive me. When I try to raise my thoughts to the Universe, there is such

convincing emptiness that those very thoughts return like sharp knives and hurt my very soul ... How painful is this unknown pain. I have no Faith. Repulsed, empty, no faith, no love, no zeal, ... What do I labor for? If there be no God, there can be no soul. If there be no soul then, Jesus, You also are not true." Would you please tell me about your feelings at that time?

Hm...

That was a test of my faith. My faith had sometimes been shaken by hardships and difficulties. Some people tried to make a profit by taking advantage of my love. It was really difficult to love such people. "To love your enemy" in the Bible was the most difficult part for me to go through at that time. The difficulties the poor gave me were not painful at all. Rather I enjoyed the difficulties. I was happy among them. But I had met many difficult situations because some people tried to make a profit by taking advantage of the poor. There were times when I reproached the Universe. It didn't protect poor and miserable people. Some people took advantage of them and even swindled them. Why did we have to suffer because of them? When I met difficult situations in which poor children had to be thrown out into the streets, I felt like reproaching Heaven.

Since I heard the voice on the train that day, God never told me anything again. When I had difficulty running the church and many facilities, I prayed. But however earnestly I prayed, the Universe didn't answer my prayers. So my faith was shaken. I had had some resentment against Heaven even for a short time then. It was more painful than anything else for my faith to be shaken before the nuns and my followers. I felt heavy and lonely because I couldn't tell anyone about that. So I stayed up so many nights shedding tears.

You had gone through a really difficult and hard time. How did you get over such difficult situations?

I overcame them with my faith too. God's love which I had sought for could be felt when I was wholeheartedly among people. I ardently love the figure of God who resides in poor people. Believing that was what God wanted me to do; I just believed and followed.

I am sometimes told that one of priests' mental sufferings is that their belief in God is often shaken. Because they have never heard the voice of God or seen Him directly, they cannot verify their belief, so they have difficulty leading their religious life from time to time. As a senior, do you have any suggestions to the priests who suffer from such difficulties?

God's figure can be opened only at the completely low places where God resides. God never stays in high and magnificent buildings. They must step down from their present positions and look for the figure of God who is shown in an extremely ordinary way. They must know that is the shortest way to meet Him. God is another expression of love. Love is indiscriminate. When they put the indiscriminate love into practice beyond any ideology and religion, they will be able to find out the holy figure of God.

Who is the God you mention?

In a broad sense, He is the one who created all things in the Universe. All things in the Universe were created by the intention of the only One, whom human beings call Buddha, God, Allah and so on according to their various cultures. The essence is one. In an accurate sense, the Creator is called the "Creator" as it is called in the Universe. The Creator called God is the father of all things in the Universe.

A lot of your work on the Earth is exemplary for people. You opened Kalighat Home for the Dying, a free hospice for the poor, the hospice Shanti Nagar (City of Peace), a home for those suffering from Hansen's disease, and the Children's Home of the Immaculate Heart, as a haven for orphans and homeless youth. You dedicated yourself to helping the helpless, the poor and the sick. What do you think of such work of yours? You opened Kalighat Home of the Dying for the poor in 1952. Why did you open that facility? What did you learn from it?

> I wanted poor people to leave the Earth with happy memories of their last moments here. It was heartbreaking that poor people suffer from poverty and hunger all their lives and then leave with the memories of the sufferings even at the moment of death. Though they had lived so, I wanted to console their souls at their last moments with our love though it was small and trivial. It was the intention of the Universe for me to carry out such work. Watching their moments of dying, I had thought a lot about death. I obtained a firm belief that I would love the Universe until the moment of death. I thought that if I loved so to my heart's content and then died, it would be a happy death.

You set up the City of Peace for the patients of Hansen disease. Did you have any difficulty setting up and running the facility?

> Hansen's disease (leprosy) causes its patients to be held in more contempt than any other disease. That disease, which is a kind of skin disease, makes the appearance of its patients very ugly and others avoid and stay away from them. So they are made to show a very servile attitude. I wanted to deliver God's love to them. I hoped for them to get over their disease for

themselves through God's love. My role was to find out God who resides at low places. That was a chance for me to grow the love within me as big as possible through the patients. I was really happy, because I was willing to do such things which other people didn't want to do. I got much help from people around rather than having any difficulty. It was difficult that society had a prejudice against them. Yet such a prejudice was not a big problem for me.

Now is the time to close our conversation. This is my last question. You had had several crises because of your heart disease. If you recovered even a little from the crises, you went to work immediately and stayed with the poor people. At last you died of the disease. What do you think of life and death?

Life is a process of putting love into practice. It is to know yourself in the process. The whole love is God's love. Human beings learn God's mind through the whole love. Human beings are born through love, live in love and finish their life with love. Love is having sympathy with all creatures. You can realize truth through the sympathy. Through my sympathy with poor people, I could realize the love of the Universe and confirm my presence. I realized through practice that the Universe is not at high or faraway places but at low places.

As for me, death was a beautiful completion. The completion of love was the very death. I loved completely until the moment of death. The Universe where you return after death is the place where you are strictly evaluated for how much you have loved yourself, for how much you have loved your neighbors and for how much you have loved the Universe. The love must originate from your whole selflessness. As

God resides where there is no self, that love is the very holy love of God. I had tried to love God with all my body and mind. The ardent love made me forget myself and God could reside there. Please love. Love so ardently that you can forget about yourself. That is another way to empty yourself.

I appreciate your touching and beautiful words.
The time I spent talking with you is so precious to me.
I really appreciate your having this conversation with
me even though you didn't have a full rest from the
fatigue of your journey to the Earth. Thank you, Marine.
Be happy.

Thank you. I had a good time recalling my life on the Earth. Good bye.

Mozart

[Wolfgang Amadeus Mozart, 1756.1.27~1791.12.5]

Today I would like to ask you about Wolfgang Ama-
deus Mozart. You already gave me much information
about him, so I'm worried about how I should lead the
interview.

Yes I know. I have been watching you.

Today, you shall meet Mozart directly in person.

What, really? I'm not quite ready yet, hold on please. Because
I feel like I should ask him about something else other than
what I had asked you before.

You don't have to find it so difficult. Just think you are having a cup of coffee with Mozart, Viennese coffee!

But still… Let's go. O.K., I will meet him.

Roar?

Is this Mozart?

Yes, I am. It's really nice to meet you. I enjoyed watching you and Marlin talking about me before.

I actually wanted to cut into your conversation but I thought it would be a breach of etiquette, so I just watched.

Wow, thanks so much for all of this. By the way, may I ask, what your name is on your planet?

It's Andria.

Ah. It has a friendly feeling. But, how should I address you?

You can call me anything you wish. You can call me Andria if you like.

I would like to call you that too, but other readers may get confused, so I will just call you by your name on the Earth. I feel that you have a bright and cheerful disposition. Your hearty laughter in the movie was quite impressive. How is your personality different from that on the Earth and on your planet?

It's so alike; it's almost identical. This personality of mine made me volunteer to go down to the Earth. I like adventure and travel, ah and I like learning. Because of this important factor I was destined to go to the Earth.

I can feel the passion in your speech, Mozart. You sound so delightful. I am kind of hesitating to ask you this question, because it might be rude. In addition to your hearty laugh, you are famous for your personality traits such as capriciousness, poor memory, etc. What made you have a personality like that?

Ha! ha! There is no special reason. When artists immerse themselves into their work, they don't really bear things in mind except their art. We can't really remember other matters. For that reason, when common people look at us, this behavior may look fastidious or reckless.

If you are a person who has experience in being absorbed in your work, you will understand this. When I'm into one thing, that is everything for me at that moment, so it's difficult to remember what I have said, thought, decided and so on. Therefore there was a difference between what I said before and what I said after time had passed, so that's why I earned a reputation like that.

I am sorry to ask you that question right off the mark.. Could I also ask you a question about what your mission on Earth was?

Sure you can. I wanted to let my Earth friends hear the music of my home planet. I expected and wished that music would touch people's spirit. Everyone here enjoys and plays music, which helps us with the balancing of our mind. I wanted to create this music on the Earth.

I really wanted to let everyone enjoy the music that transcends all class, without any discrimination.

So then, your music should be described as the music of the Universe, not as the music of the Earth.

Does it sound like that?

Yes, that's exactly how people comment on your music; they say it is the music of the Universe not the music of Earth.

Wow, really? That's a very generous comment. The comments of Earth people about me are so excessive, it makes me blush.

You said you wanted to communicate and heal people through your music. When people listen to your music, they say they don't feel like it's communication between humans,

they feel like it's communication between the universe and humans or with one's soul.

Which part of a human did you intend to communicate to, through your music?

> I used music as an instrument to purify humans' mind. But if its contents express normal human emotion, then it wouldn't perform its function properly. As you said, my music was the tool to help human beings feel the wave of the Universe, not the wave of the world of mortals. Through the music, I wanted humans to communicate with the Universe, to purify themselves, and especially to let them experience the process of emptying their emotions which were in a negative spiral.

I see. Actually music is entirely outside my field, but if my musician friends find out I'm talking to Mozart, they would really be jealous! I feel I should give you their greetings too. Once after I heard your music in a movie, it made me buy your record. And your music even made me want to learn to play a musical instrument.

> Oh wow! Thank you so much. I feel as if I could fly.

Likewise, your music was like a haven to many people on Earth, especially to the people who were experiencing difficulties with their emotions. I think every part of your music exudes love towards humans. I think that because you had the love toward humans, you hoped for humans to be healed and communicate with the universe through your art. In the case of many other artists, they often struggled from their own agony, so they sublimated this process into their work. But, your art work does not really deal with the pain of personal life, rather, every element of your art contains the love toward humans.

> You're very generous with your compliments. If my music was useful like that, I'm as happy as can be.

Through music we can meet our own self, nature, and the Universe. One of the reasons why I went to Earth was to share the music of the universe with the people. And it was because I wished that I could fill and warm people's hearts with that music, just a little.

By the way, I think that on the one hand you received so much love from the world, but on the other hand your music has been used too much for commercial gain.

Honestly I'm indifferent. If my music is played to the people, no matter where or in which situation, if people find even a little solace and enjoyment from it, that gives me supreme happiness and it is a gift from the artist. No matter which way they use my music, it means they have the intention of playing that music to others, and because they also have the concept of love, it is possible.

Ah, you are right. By the way, when you were on the Earth, did you know you were originally a cosmic being?

No I didn't know. But, when I was working on my music I never knew my melodies would flow out so naturally. It was truly a wonderful experience, even for me. Those unusual experiences kept me going. It was an endless moment of happiness. And in addition, the public paid attention to my music and through this they were happy, so for me, watching them feeling happiness was a great motivation.

Wow, so awesome. When you were born on the Earth, did you choose a particular home environment?

Yes, my top priority was the environment where I could create my music without rein.

I chose circumstances where I could quickly discover and develop my talent. Even now, I have a disposition that really dislikes being bound and tied down to something. Aren't you the same?

Yes, I'm a lot like that too. However, it seems, your father, Leopold, restrained you a lot. Even though he gave you wholehearted support, your relationship seems to have been a love-hate one. Is this something you had also chosen?

It was a kind of stabilizer. If I had planned my life extremely freely, it would've been somewhat difficult to practice my mission. But my father took the role of restraining me in some things; so I could have a fast pace and stability in order to present my ability.

Accordingly, my father is a very important person who helped me to practice my mission from a young age. He came to the Earth to play such role. But, because of my genius, even though he truly had unconditional love for his child, he also couldn't help being envious of my ability, therefore he agreed to come to Earth to study humility through me. And I had established the firm footing of a family environment for performing my mission. Also, I had restriction in my life from my father. This in fact, made a good environment for me to concentrate on music, and it was an excellent way not to waste energy on other things; we both had agreed upon this. Consequently, we both were helpful to each other, but we also both gave restrictions to each other and provided an environment to study other aspects.

I see. Do you still have contact with your father? My question is so random, isn't it?

No, it is fun. Unfortunately, no, I don't. My relationship with him is quite substantial, but currently we both play our role in our own place, and we don't connect because, my father is on another planet right now.

Your father was also a cosmic being. You were a cosmic being family.

Yes.

You like traveling very much, don't you? So, you took a very long trip to the Earth. I know that after you were born on Earth, you also traveled a lot .

Travel allows us to experience a lot. For me, travel was the process that helped me receive the wave from my home planet successfully. Through travel, I could learn about myself faster. I learned about musical talent and the passion for music that I had on my planet. Through travel, I aroused the process of realizing my genius … If I had not travelled, I couldn't have developed my talent that fast. This is another reason why I had arranged the family relationship with my father. He noticed my talent very quickly, and in order to cultivate that talent, he gave me complete support and spared no effort, there wasn't anything left for my father at the end, as he only lived his life for me.

Yes, it seems so. I think the love of a parent towards their child on the Earth is really amazing.

May I ask you, which was the most memorable place on Earth that you travelled to?

I liked Venice in Italy so much.

Ah, yes. The glasswork is really pretty there. By the way, can I ask you about your relationship with Salieri?

He was a good rival for me. There was a lot I could learn from him. He was a great man who achieved

222 The Universe Speaks

everything only through his effort. In some ways, I was not a fair rival. I received the wave from my planet, and also the ability I already had from before just flowed out so naturally. Whereas, Salieri only accomplished his music through ceaseless effort, how could I not admire him? He might have been hurt by my fastidious and rough personality, but that also was to give him conditions to learn humility.

A genius is often egocentric and has little interest in looking at others. It's because the rival for the genius, is himself. They are always craving and wondering about something from inside of themselves. Expecting a genius to love and pay warm attention to their surroundings could be quite a difficult matter, because they already experience difficulty from the pain and overwhelming burden that comes from their existence itself. Salieri was so envious of my genius. He had to accept the presence of the genius itself, but he endlessly compared himself to it.

We are all very different. There is no superiority or inferiority. Each human being who is born, is created in the image of God, to be loved and is so precious in themselves. But humans constantly compare themselves with someone else. And they are tormented by a thirst and desire for things they don't have. Salieri represents such a human character.

It not only speaks of the part of being jealous of a genius and suffering from the fact that he can't be like that, it also speaks of another human characteristic where people become estranged from their original nature and try to find themselves through relationships with others. It shows how exhausting and unnecessary such thinking and living is.

On Earth, humans often try to judge and measure themselves through comparison, but that is a very unusual concept on our planet. Here, we don't compare ourselves, we judge ourselves according to ourselves. What is considered most important is the evaluation based on the plan we make for ourselves.

In conclusion, what I want to tell Earth people is that all human beings are so precious and it's not advisable to evaluate yourself through comparing oneself to others. What's important is how much you love and enjoy your work.

The loving heart of the Creator, that wishes all humans to learn the way to love themselves, is embedded everywhere.

Thank you for your great words. I really needed those words. How others think about me has always bothered me… It's not so easy to break away from those thoughts while living on Earth.

Yes, I know because I was born there too. I know how difficult it is.

Then, can I ask you about a lighter topic? You got married on Earth. How was your married life?

Marriage on Earth was not what I had planned. For the practicing of my mission, earthly marriage could, in a sense, have been an obstacle.

An obstacle? Oh dear.

Did my expression sound negative? I will correct it then. I'll say it wasn't really necessary. But, when

I looked around after being born, marriage was such a huge matter. Everyone wanted to get married, and it was considered as a natural consequence. It looked very funny to me.

Then, what does marriage mean to you?

Artists are very emotional people. The process of creating a piece of art from the various emotions is similar to the process of the carving of jewels. It was the same for me. I chose marriage because it gave me the conditions that allowed me to relax from the spiraling of my emotions. I had lived a public life since I was a child, which mostly consisted of traveling with my father and musical activities, that I hardly had a childhood. Therefore, I pursued marriage as the means to become independent from my father.

Oh, that's quite a dangerous idea.

Yeah, right? Haha. But a variety of factors conspired to make me choose marriage. But my marriage was not an unhappy one. Both marriage and having children were different experiences for me on Earth.

I see. In what way?

On my planet, the marriage institution is not rigid. It is very flexible. It is not a concept of ownership or restriction. But marriage on Earth, included such indescribable concepts. It's like a gateway for two independent individuals to become one. Marriage on our planet is the encounter through which we help each other as independent individuals who have the same purpose.

If so then it doesn't include love?

Love is basic. But, thinking of the other as yours and mine is not the concept of love. It is the love, which acknowledges another's existence itself, as it is. Our marriage institution supports each individual to perform their duty well. So I didn't have a plan to get married when I came down to Earth, but after years of living on Earth, I wanted to experience what an Earth marriage is like. At that precise moment, I met Constanze, such a beautiful spirit. She is a beautiful woman who provided me with the experience of the flow of human emotions. With eternal gratitude I thank her.

If you could put the marriage in the universe in one word, what would it be?

It is "beautiful encounter". It is an independent union without wanting anything from each other, and even just being around each other, is a wholehearted support for the other's mission.

That is really great. Are you married on your planet?

No.

Are you missing Constanze?

Oh, you got me... Haha, it was a beautiful experience. I still keep in contact with Constanze sometimes, because we are on the same planet.

Wow, that sounds interesting…

Yes, I know.

What would you like to say about your life on earth? You lived a brief life, only until the age of 36.

It was an exciting and unusual experience. It was fun. Honestly, my home planet is a quiet and serene planet, so from time to time I still miss the life on the Earth. I look around there sometimes and reminisce about those times.

But the reason why I chose a short life is because I practiced my calling from my childhood, so it wasn't necessary to stay longer. If I had displayed my talent from my adolescence, I could have lived longer. Because I might have needed more time to perform my role. People, who come because of a calling, choose their time to go back.

Does that mean, you knew you came from the Universe?

No, it wasn't like that. If I say, at the point of my death, I felt, 'I have got to go back to the place where I came from', would you believe it?

Actually, many people feel sorry about your short life. Would you like to born again on Earth?

nope…

Uh, that's an unexpected answer.

Earth has changed so much from when I went there. So I don't really have a wish to do that.

That's too bad. If your fans heard you were coming down again, they would be excited. But, yes, you are right. The Earth has become polluted and has been destroyed so much.

You are a very well-known person to us Earth people. What is your best memory from your life on Earth?

My sons.

Ah, right, I heard you had two sons.

I think that it is only on Earth that you have the opportunity to experience marriage and having children. Because I had them, I could experience a personal side of life. Also, it makes me remember my life on Earth as a happy one.

Yes, I guess your experience of being a parent left you with a deep impression.

Yes, it's a beautiful experience. As a parent, the emotion of love towards children was truly a precious experience. When I think about humans, the love of parents towards their children is a highly purified love that no one and nowhere in the Universe can possibly match. But of course, the way of loving is very important. Love that is blinded and inconsiderate of others is far from what I mean.

I've seen that you and your family often corresponded with each other. Particularly, there are a lot of opinions about your letters to your cousin. People suspect that it may not have been purely a relationship of just cousins...

Is that what they are really saying? My cousin was a wholehearted supporter of me. When I was going through tough times mentally and emotionally, she consoled me. She always looked after me as a counselor. I was able to share everything with my cousin, which means I was in close communication with her. Because she was there, I felt less isolated while living my life.

I consider the sort of relationship that people are talking about as only an excessive interest in me, the interest about the celebrity. This is also something to be thankful for. If people take an interest in me through that rumor and get to encounter my music, this is also another way to perform my role.

The reason why I could be close to my cousin is because it was very difficult to live a stable life due to my frequent travels. In that situation, it is so hard to maintain a friendship. And so, even though we were cousins, we maintained a strong friendship and communicated at all times.

Ah, so that is the reason. It seems like you must have been lonely. Rather than having normal relationships for your age, you just got immersed in music and didn't have room to enjoy small, ordinary fun that life can give us. Oh, I am sorry for you.

That was just the pre-arranged schedule of my life.

Oh schedule... I see it was not so easy. By the way, what do you think the meaning of music is?

Music is the instrument that can touch a person's soul. It is a tool that can form a bridge which connects a human to their inner world. In many cases, humans are too far removed from their original self to know it. However, music leads people to their innocent, original mind. The reason why I came to the Earth with music as my specialty, is because I wanted humans to hear music that can do that.

In other words, I wanted to help people meet their true selves. I would like to call it communication and healing. It was such an honorable and happy role for me that I was able to visit the Earth; that I was able to carry out what I planned and that I experienced the life as a human being while doing all of this. These were the happiest moments in my life.

According to music therapists, more than 60% of your compositions consist of high frequency sounds of more than 3,000 to 4,000Hz. Tinnitus or conductive and sensor neural hearing loss can be improved if people listen to your music, since the sensitivity of sensory nerves become enhanced. Also, mind calming hormones such as serotonin and acetylcholine are secreted, so high blood pressure can be lowered. When people hear your music, parasympathetic nerves are activated and one's body and mind

become comfortable and conditions can be improved. Can I ask you about this?

Humans enjoy analyzing things. It is a bit awkward to talk about it myself, but the waves that flow from my music comfort people. It is such a gratifying thing that my music can give numerous people comfort throughout many centuries.

The world of waves is so beautiful. It is amazing that all kinds of communications are possible with the motion of waves. Music is one of the means through which beings can communicate using waves without borrowing the power of language. Artists or people who are familiar with and enjoy music can more easily and quickly communicate with the universe because they have acquired and utilized the methods of how to communicate through waves even without their knowledge.

Then, the waves your music carries are passed on to people and they are purified automatically, correct?

Yes, that is the same for all kinds of arts. What kinds of waves an artist loads on his/her art piece determines what waves people who meet the works of art will receive. I am so grateful for the fact that my compositions contain the waves that can purify human emotion. In this way, everything is delivered and received through waves like the way we are conversing with each other now.

Yes, that is so brilliant. You have dealt with almost all genres of music from vocal to instrumental music and you composed various types of music such as chamber music, concerto, symphony, opera and so on. Which is your favorite genre?

I prefer chamber music. Although each genre has its own charm, personally I love chamber music that doesn't need much formality therefore anyone can naturally enjoy it. I also like solemn and majestic music, but I love music that can comfort my mind.

By the way, since the Earth is in the material world, various musical instruments are used to create music. I am wondering about how music is made in the Universe. I guess the ways can differ on each planet just as each region on Earth has its own traditional instruments.

Cosmic beings also have musical instruments. They are different from material ones, though. We can make and play musical instruments whenever we want. We don't carry musical instruments as the people on the Earth do. We can play them when we need them. However, it is not the case for all planets. Depending on the grade of the planet, their instrument may exist in the material form like on Earth or on other planets, they may not. The higher a planet's grade is, the less the need for materials, so they create as much as they need and obtain things in various ways on the spot.

What kinds of musical instruments does your planet have?

They are not so different from those of the human world. That is because musical instruments played by the Earth's human beings are also mostly from the Universe.

A human being himself is a musical instrument. The ways to express oneself can vary. Both the player and the listener can be purified while playing or listening to the music. This is the reason why the role of artists is so important and also beautiful. In the case of the Earth, people regard art as a high level of technique and only expect privileged talents to perform it.

However, the process of overcoming such a fixed idea can be the opportunity to empty and grow oneself.

An opportunity to empty and grow oneself?

It generally refers to any fixed ideas you have. It is not just limited to arts.

What musical instrument did you like?

I loved the piano. Whenever I saw my fingers beating down the piano keys like dancing, I was in high spirits. In those moments, only I existed. I even forgot about the fact the audience was listening to me play. For me, every moment is a time of gratitude. I handled musical instruments I loved and people got comfort and joy, listening to the music; it was such a happy moment.

Then, do you have any messages you want to pass on to those who study music?

All of those who make music are born with a mission. Although they are seeking to fulfill personal desire, what they truly want inside is to make people of the world happy with their music. In the course of pursuing music they may encounter their own limitations and suffer from hard times; but that is the life process towards happiness and evolution for the musician. They have a mystical power that can make people's emotions happy, sad or hard. I hope they won't forget about this. I wish them to trust their own power and create music that can soothe and heal people's minds.

That is why a musician him/herself must be happy. I wish them to have the power of mind to cultivate their inner being to be pure, bright and warm. They can't forget that they are loved and blessed beings only for the one thing, that they can make people happy with their instrument of music. They should know that only when they love themselves, and are able to make people happy, can they create music that can give strength to people.

Musicians go through the process of evolution through the means of music, don't they?

Music makes a powerful tool for evolution. This course is a challenge for infinity; one is supposed to confront one's limitation. The process is, consequently, that of humility and selflessness. It means that the moment comes when one realizes that the talent and the ability they thought was their own, is actually not. In fact, there is nothing they can do. Nevertheless, the reason why they keep striving and creating is because it makes them happy. Even though they bump against their limitations, they are driven to seek music by a sense of fulfillment that accomplishment gives them. However, it is not the case only for musicians. Not only artists but also all human beings have the same experience. Through the works they do, they go through the three attributes for evolution: pain, encounter and boredom, and then through the process they ultimately reach evolution. In the case of artists, as their work process is outwardly evident, although the degree looks a bit more intensive, we can view all the activities we perform as art.

I am afraid I'm going to ask you a bit of a difficult question. Your death seems to be such a secret that people say it is a mystery. Can I ask about Mozart's death? I heard that you wrote the "Requiem" on your sickbed until the moment of your death.

For human beings, life and death are quite big issues. I went through such an experience. My life was focused on music and showing my personal characteristics was only viewed as the eccentric deeds of a genius musician and I rarely had the chance to have human bonds. I can say I was fussy and temperamental because I didn't have a normal childhood. I achieved success in music from my childhood and my musical achievements gave joy to people; however we can see it was a hard course for me as an individual.

Nonetheless, life on the Earth was such an interesting and amusing experience. Mentally and emotionally, I had many difficulties, however the fact that I completed my mission and that my music has lasted for several centuries as a light for the world, is very gratifying. I didn't want my death to become an issue for people. I just wanted to complete my life quietly. I was also exhausted with life on Earth. My death happened the way I had chosen, I found out about this after I passed away. By the way, what do you think about the fact that we are conversing with each other in this way?

What do you mean?

I am the one who has already died, but you are conversing with me like this.

Oh, that is right.

Death is just changing dimensions. Taking off one's physical body and moving to another dimension. Just as I wrapped up my life on the Earth, cast off my clothes of the life on the Earth, i.e. the physical body and returned to my home planet, each person is designed to shift to other dimensions after death. You must be curious about what kind of dimension it will be; it will be determined by the evaluation of the life you had.

On the Earth, in fact, death is something fearful. It is also a taboo topic.

Yes, I know. I also had such an experience. I experienced the fear and anxiety of death which swooped down on me while I was writing my last work.

How did you get over it?

I came to know naturally. The fact that death is the process of moving on to the next world based on the evaluation about my life… So I was able to pass away comfortably.

I understand. The conversation became slightly heavy. Here comes a personal question. Can I ask how old you are? It is O.K. if you don't want to answer.

I am about thirty thousand years old.

Wow, I can't imagine.

This is just a norm in the Universe.

I see. Although we are in the same Universe, things are so different. Can I ask you for your last message you want to send to the people of the Earth?

My life on the Earth is a beautiful memory. The Earth is such a beautiful planet in the Universe. I don't know how I can express my feelings of appreciation for the beautiful people's love for my music. However I would like to tell you that the Earth is not a place which exists only for human beings. All the members of the universe have a common destiny. I need you to value and love the Earth like you love my music.

Thank you. Andria…

William Shakespeare

I would like to ask you about William Shakespeare. What was his mission on the Earth?

His mission was to study human emotions. Through his plays and acting, he wanted to show people what emotions were which turn you completely upside down or sometimes lead you to evolve when you get through them. He studied human emotions and wrote dramas based on the result. He showed Earth people the emotional world of one's inner side that is far from one's original self, but which can determine one's life.

He did it because he wanted to give people the opportunity to look back on themselves and learn something from the diverse human characters that appear in his dramas. People make a self-portrait from the actors and actresses acting on stage. Shakespeare wished people would realize the essence of something they are pursuing. It can be money, honor or sex. Eventually, his role was to study human emotions and describe the studied emotions in this plays so that Earth people can reflect on themselves as they are while watching his plays. He wished people to evolve themselves through this process.

Then, what is his role in his home planet? Do you have writers on your planet?

He still studies human emotions – the emotions of people of his planet and the meaning and role of emotions in the Universe. Oh, of course we have writers. We are all artists as well as mind healers. In fact, we are all writers too. Yet each of us has our own specialized area.

I watched a film on Shakespeare once. It was fun. I read a book about him too.

Yeah, I have been watching you trying to understand Shakespeare. You know what?

Yes?

Shakespeare was also watching you searching for information about him.

Oh, really? I didn't expect that, so I feel a bit embarrassed.

No, we were happy. He is waiting for you now.

Thank you.

Yes, then here you go.

Hi, Roar.

Are you Shakespeare?

Ha ha…! Yes I am.

I watched a movie about you, so you are familiar to me.

As you feel familiar with me, too. It is nice to meet you.

If I had majored in English literature, we would be able to talk deeply about your work.

It doesn't matter because we know a lot about each other already.

Then, let me start with a mild question. Did you have a particular reason why you chose Europe, especially England?

The main reason is due to language. In order to come close to people, the language I use should have been an easy and simple one for the public. English is spoken by most people in the world. I chose England because the power of English was the major factor.

And there is one more reason. It is the characteristic of Britain. British people loved plays. All the people were interested in plays or dramas and loved them.

Really? I thought England was a conservative and closed country.

As she is a conservative country, people prefer to express their feelings indirectly through plays. In an open society, people can express their feelings as they feel, but in a conservative society people need a tool that can express their feelings on behalf of them. So you can see it as people revealing their feelings through plays in a theater.

I understand. That is why British plays are famous. Well... I guess it became so because you were there.

Do you think so?

Yes, of course. You are one of the greatest playrights in world history and you were the most powerful one. You are called 'the leading figure of English literature'. It is like a dream that I can actually talk with you.

I am so flattered. Thank you very much.

You know what? I would really wish to read your pieces of work once again if I had much more time. Ah, I also listen to Mozart a lot.

You do?

I guess one of the reasons that made English so powerful globally even now is because you were born in Britain and left many beautiful pieces in English. By the way, your personal life remains mysterious. It is said that you married very young. Did you get married?

Yes, I did. I was in a burning love when I was still very young and I married her. When I look back to my life on Earth now, I was incorrigible and naughty. Yet, it was such a grateful experience. You know, it is so dramatic that you can only experience it on the Earth. Marriage on the Earth is a system where you can experience all human emotions in a short period. I was engulfed in those magical powers and got married. I had a burning love; married a woman but we became estranged later on. In that process, I got through all the emotions that humans have completely. This made a foundation that greatly influenced my writing activity as a result.

Hmm...I am not sure whether I can ask you this, but was it a marriage planned by you before your birth on the Earth?

No, never. One of the things I experienced while living as an Earth human was that it was so hard to control my emotions. At that time I was a vigorous youth and I played with love. Yet, I do not regret it. It was a great experience. But, I feel sorry for concentrating only on my work. I did not care about my family. You know marriage is a system that demands a lot of effort and sacrifice. I didn't think about them much.

I see. What was the most exciting experience you had on Earth?

I liked the whole process where I felt human emotions and then expressed them in my writing. It was a lot of fun. I was so thankful for my role that I actually played on stage with the dramas I wrote. It was like I showed my emotions to the entire world on a stage called the Earth.

I feel you are very lively and humorous. I can feel your lively energy when you talk.

Ha ha ha! Please receive as much as you want of it. Well... My life on Earth was a very happy experience for me. It is also fun to compare emotions on Earth and emotions on my planet and study both. You know what? As I lived on the Earth, I am now able to understand the human emotions and explain them well. I am actually the first one who can do so.

Wow! You are cool. I guess you might teach people who wish to come down on Earth on your planet?

How did you guess? Perhaps it was possible because you were connected to the waves of the Universe. Cosmic beings that are going to the Earth take lessons about the Earth. Among the programs they take, I am in charge of human emotions. When you go down to the Earth, you forget everything – like where you are from, why you are there and so on. Yet the information you receive from the lessons would help you anyway.

Oh, I see. That is really interesting.

Yes. You know, it is such a great adventure for cosmic beings to decide a life on Earth. It is an exciting journey. Therefore, you need to prepare for it well. You need to learn many things. There are many subjects to take. My part is human emotions and it belongs to a subject, "How to get along well with humans". I give information on diverse and mysterious human emotions.

Mr. Shakespeare! You are an expert on the emotions of cosmic beings as well as Earth people, right?

Ha haha!… I am not that good.

Don't be shy. You know you are great. That is why you were able to produce such masterpieces. You know better about human emotions than us humans. The human emotions you illustrated in your tragic or comic dramas fill out the aspects people are not even aware of themselves.

I really enjoyed my work. I am so thankful that I was given such an opportunity. As I returned to my planet after I completed my mission on the Earth, I got more interested in human emotions and watched the Earth. I fell in love with the Earth even more deeply; including those I worked and lived with there.

(His telepathic wave tells me he misses his life on Earth.)
You seem to have loved your life on Earth a lot.

The Earth... it is such a beautiful planet. You cannot help loving it. It is one of the most beautiful planets of the Universe because it is in harmony with nature. Do you believe that many cosmic beings who once lived on Earth feel so sorry about the Earth now?

Oh, really? I feel ashamed and sorry.

I am one of many cosmic beings who support the Earth, a beautiful planet in the Universe. I hope Earth people would recognize that the Earth does not only belong to Earth people. It is actually a part of the Universe. I study human emotions because I wanted to help them spend their emotions on loving and giving thanks to each other, not wasting them on hating or envying others. I demonstrated to them through my dramas after I watched human emotions carefully.

I wished people to purify their minds a little bit when they watch my plays. I wanted them to purify their minds and change their action. Can you believe that changes of each one's emotions actually affect the entire Universe through waves?

Are we all connected to that extent? I thought one's emotions are only limited to oneself.

It is not true. Even though we are so distant from each other, we are able to talk through waves. Like this, human emotions can be sent to a star which is far from the Earth through waves. If you can deliver waves of joy, you will make the Universe happier. If you send waves of sadness, then the Universe will become sadder.

I see, Mr. Shakespeare. So you are not an isolated individual, but have no option but to get connected as a member of the Universe.

Yes. We are all part of the Universe and we form a group that shares a common destiny.

Wow…as I converse with you, I come to understand a secret of the Universe. You know, it feels like I am dreaming even if I talk to you in person like this. I am even more surprised to hear that we are one.

Yes, do you also feel that? The Universe has a lot of information – you cannot imagine how much, and we are all connected.

Here comes the next question. It is about your appearance. People say they cannot guarantee that that is your portrait in which you are bald, wear earrings and have a mustache. There are a lot of rumors regarding how you really looked. What did you look like?

Ha ha ha! That is an interesting question. Actually that *is* my portrait.

Oh, is it?

I wasn't particularly interested in leaving my portrait, but it was a social custom. It only made the most of my characteristics. Why? Are you disappointed?

Oops! Did you notice?

You must be expecting someone who is much better-looking.

Well… this image came up with me when I thought about you. What kind of an actor were you? Contemporary actors or actresses are not just actors or actresses. They are even regarded as idols. What was an actor like in your time? When I watched a movie about you, people of your time wanted to become actors and they enjoyed writing.

People in the middle class wanted to become actors in those days. Well…I chose to be an actor for a living, but what is more important is that I wanted to understand a drama deeply and to write plays while acting on a stage in the meantime. It was such an exciting experience to have played on stage as an actor.

Especially, the preparation to be on stage is a very joyous as well as a beautiful one. Actors and staff members become one and complete a drama. It is a very attractive process. When all those who participate in the process play their roles perfectly, it makes a drama on stage shine and the feeling you have is great. If you cannot become one with others in a group, no matter how wonderful a play is, you cannot attract the audience.

A characteristic of Europe, especially England is that this country has a strong fondness for art. Partly it is because people do not express their feelings straightforwardly. That social atmosphere usually also made people of that country like writing and acting. Yet, people in the upper class do not think highly of actors. They regard them as people who entertain them.

I see. I guess you might have been a romantic and shrewd person. Ah, and a boaster too!

Ha ha! Do you feel so? 80% is correct. I was obstinate and incorrigible too. As a matter of fact, I liked my disposition of that time.

I see. Do you have actors or actresses on your home planet?

Yes, we do.

Oh really?

Yes, of course. We are all artists as well as actors or actresses, especially people in charge of art meditation. They are all artists, actors or actresses. In my planet too, there are theaters, actors and actresses. We regularly present plays on a stage. You know, it is a kind of theater group run by each project. Therefore, we do not present plays regularly but do so when it is necessary. We form a group to play on a stage in a short time, practice and present a play on a stage.

I feel our conversation has been wrapped in mystery. I also feel like I am making up a story now.

Everyone feels so when he/she converses with me. There are diverse dramas. The main stream is what the emotion of people on other planets is like and how we should control emotion to steer it in the direction of evolution; and we present it as a play. Especially regarding the emotion of Earth people, I am an expert, so I deliver amusement together with information to many cosmic beings all over the Universe who are interested in the evolution of the Earth. I have my plays on the stage too.

I don't know where our talk is heading. I want to watch your plays someday. By the way, what is your favorite play? What do you prefer between tragedy and comedy?

I like sonnets. Writing plays is fun, but I like poems more because they can contain everything, even if they are short. Sometimes it sounds like singing. You know, the charm of Earth's language is enshrined.

That's wonderful. I just looked into one of sonnets that you wrote. I want to receive your writing if I am good at receiving waves from you but I will pass this time.
Your four tragedies and five comedies were made into many films or TV shows. They were played as you wrote them or sometimes they were modified according to the trend of each era. What do you think of those?

I enjoyed watching them. You did too, right? When I observe the history of the Earth, human interest has a certain pattern. It is a bit different for each time or region but in the long term they are the same. Emotions are the same too. It seems like there are a variety of emotions but when you look into one's emotions deeply, there are not many. You know the seven emotions. Those emotions led the history of the Earth.

Human desires and emotions do not change and so my dramas can be re-played in various time backgrounds. Ah, I will give you an answer to your question. I prefer comedy to tragedy. It is suitable for my disposition. I don't really like something serious. It is much more fun to impress people through comedy. Tragedy is a direct expression. I satirized periphrastically.

When a play ends with someone's death, it can have a direct effect on the audience but it won't last long. It is because people avoid relating it to their own lives. Maybe some might say people would just laugh about comedy and that is all but comedy sinks into one's life slowly. You would like to connect your current life situation to a comedy. I wanted to pursue such fun.

I see. Thank you. This question is a bit heavy. Some speak about an inscription on your tombstone. Is that something you wrote?

Yes, I did it myself. My job is writing so I wrote many articles. As a matter of fact, I didn't intend it to be on my tombstone. My acquaintances found it and presumed that I had written it for that purpose and so they inscribed it into my tombstone.

What do you think of people's new viewpoint on your epitaph? You wrote, "Good friend, please do not dig my dust..." People see it as you criticizing iconolatry.

Ha ha ha ha I find it interesting. No, I didn't mean that. It is a broad interpretation. Sometimes people discover things that even writers didn't think about. You know critics. However…. it is true that I did mean it somehow. I was worried about the people of my era becoming idol worshippers. By the time I was near to completing my mission on the Earth, I wanted people to learn lessons from my dramas. I didn't want people to become interested in my personal life. I meant that when I wrote it. In fact, there is nothing religious in it. To be more specific, it was rather about myself. Well… but it can be applied to religions, I guess.

Lastly, may I ask you for some words for writers on Earth?

First of all I would like to thank you on behalf of writers. They are those who have the precious talent of impressing people and changing their minds so that the world can become a little bit more pure, bright and warm. Therefore, I want them to love themselves first and to be happy. Love yourself first and when you have a happy mind, it will overflow from your mind and you will write beautifully. This will lighten up the world. All those writers in the world, please go for it!

Thank you.

Chapter 13

A Beautiful Universe

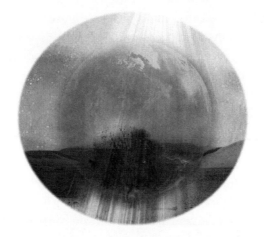

Characteristics of Planets and Stars of Different Levels

I have meditated on the Universe. When I look into a night sky, there are a number of stars. I cannot imagine how all of them were created. Then an idea came across my mind: just like my body is composed of surprisingly many cells, the Universe is maybe composed up of stars, which are like the cells in my body.

Galaxies or clusters of stars are also acting like cells or groups of cells in the Universe.

An ecosystem of one's body, nature or the Universe is not different but they are actually one and so human beings are called, "small universes."

I don't need to think of the Universe as a grand and broad space but consider it like myself. Sometimes I love it, hate it, and accept it or not.

However, the Universe is not something that can be replaced with another because it is like myself. When I think of the Universe like that, I feel it's closer.

Maybe it must be the Creator's will as to why it was created.

Then... I would like to hear about planets and stars today.

A planet or star is life.

It is a foundation for life.

It is a foundation where lives can dwell and grow.

They have generating substances that can be transformed into a 3rd dimensional existence as the universe energy descends and is harmonized with it. A jewel that is made of concentrated energy for a long time; that is a star. A star is a crystal of energy.

A jewel is the first element. When a jewel is combined with another and refined, it turns into the second element. After it goes through the 3rd and 4th transformations, it turns into a crystal of energy, that is a crystal of mental energy. It is a star that is formed by combining those crystals.

A complex planet like the Earth, required dozens of elements, including the Five Elements in the solar system.

In order to have various experiments with such diverse life forms so as to be called the exhibition hall of life diversity of the Universe, the Earth needs to be made with the various kinds of energy and connected to such energy lines.

The amount of vital energy is set up by the usage of the planet or the star.

Vital energy determines the speed of evolution.

Next let me ask you now about stars or planets of different levels from grade 1 through to grade 10.

Haha, I understand. You are better off browsing them once. Are you O.K. with it?

Sure, will I view them visually?

Kind of… It would be appropriate if we call it 5D. You don't visit them in person but you can see and feel them vividly. It is a bit dangerous that you go there firsthand because in fact it is not allowed yet.

O.K., I don't mind. Didn't you say stars or planets of level 1-3 are made of pure substances, right?

Yes. The planets you see now are pure substances existing in the solar system.

They look like salt crystals.

They are planets. You may think so because they look small. Then let's magnify them.

It looks like diverse planets with no living beings spread in each planetary system.

Think of the Milky Way.

It is water.

What is water like?

You might think the ocean is empty. Several islands are floating in the ocean and some fish and seaweed live in there but the ocean itself is filled with water molecules.

The density is different thus you feel it is vacant.

It is the same for the Universe.

The Universe, which is the great ocean, is filled with emptiness.

In the Universe there are stars, planets, living things and floating creatures sparsely scattered.

It is not vacant but it looks so because it is terribly huge.

Substances that have filled the Universe tightly circulate and exchange information and density for a long period of time. It is like the emptiness is nothing other than form or form is nothing other than emptiness. Over a long period time, like electrons exchange, things change over and over again.

As it takes too much time, it looks as though it takes forever.

You know, to a child, an hour of waiting seems like eternity but to an adult you can guess what time it is because you have a watch.

The inanimate planets you see around the solar system are grade 2 or 3.

Planets of grade 1 are at the core of the Universe. Those planets supply raw substances for all kinds of energy. Like the Amazon should be preserved on the Earth, those planets should be protected as well.

Even though you mix paints on a color palette, you have stored original paints. Therefore, you can make the original color anytime.

Such work has been done repeatedly in each star, galaxy and Universe.

The cycle of the great Universe has experienced that too.

You know what, level 3 or level 6 is like how much paints and water are mixed on a palette.

The way to thin paste with water or mix paints are how all creations in the Universe evolve and how the Creator exists.

Such process exists for everlasting evolution.

Inanimate planets and stars around the Earth do not have any living creatures yet have a lot of vital energy.

They are connected to the core of the Earth through lines and supply energy to the Earth.

However, the line has a problem now.

The valve of the line is controlled depending on how the Earth would turn out.

This will affect the Earth when the Earth enters a period of great change, the photon belt.

It's a bit difficult to understand.

I never heard about such things.

May I look into the planets more closely?

Some are big. When those planets that are made of energy become noticeable to people's eyes, then people can reside on them?

Yes. They have vital energy. They are now used for a specific purpose, i.e., to preserve such energy, but when the location and the energy line change, those planets will be promoted to a higher grade.

I see. Is the Earth the only planet of the 3ʳᵈ dimension in the entire solar system?

> For now the solar system is in the 3ʳᵈ dimension. When the solar system passes through the photon belt, this system will be promoted to a higher dimension.

I understand. Then the 4ᵗʰ dimensional world is only surrounding the Earth?

> Yes. The 4ᵗʰ dimensional world reveals the imperfection of the Earth; the realm of materials and the Realm of Spirit that can never get mixed with each other. Spiritual beings in the 4ᵗʰ dimension evolve more slowly than people in the 3ʳᵈ dimension, but they evolve faster than those in the 5ᵗʰ dimension.

> Even in the Realm of Spirit, you have a lot to learn.

> The best way is to learn as much as you can while you can, earning lessons from your life while you have your a physical body.

> No matter how long you learn, it is very difficult to be awakened.

> Thus, people choose to be born again eventually so that they can continue their study.

> But this is only possible for those who are somehow enlightened.

Where is the closest planet or star of the 5ᵗʰ dimension?

Is that planet a Utopia, which we have heard about in myths or legend?

> A place that is called "Utopia" to people belongs to the 4ᵗʰ dimension.

> You know it is a villa of the 4ᵗʰ dimension realized on the Earth.

Yet, from Earth people's viewpoint, the upper layer of the Realm of Spirit would look like a paradise, because life on earth is almost contrary to that...

O.K. Maybe the world higher than that must be more beautiful and nicer. I don't know how to express it though.

Well... but it might not look so different.

It is a matter of one's mind.

You know, a clean canvas is not always good even though it is blank.

If a painter gives it one stroke with his brush, then the common canvas turns into a billion-dollar treasure.

A high dimensional planet is a place where writers with good-will live and create art that is called life.

When the good-will has been accumulated, such a high dimension will be maintained.

The leaders of those planets should maintain the condition and develop it.

There is only one thing that they are more excellent at.

They know relatively better.

They know where to go and how to get there.

Thus, all they do in a planet for evolution becomes the activities of politics, economics and art.

All right. Then what is different about a 5th dimensional planet compared to a 6th dimensional planet?

The difference is about whether you have a physical body or not.

The 5th dimension includes both sides, therefore we call it a semi-ether body.

Thus, it's possible to practice training[1] methods that requires the condition of having a body.

But the function of the danjeon is different from what you have now.

For the physical human being, the danjeon is the only channel for the world beyond the body.

When you become semi-ether, your entire body will become the danjeon, so you will be able to do training throughout your entire body.

Acupoints and meridians in your body will be always opened, thus there is no need to accumulate energy anymore, but you will just use it by procuring it whenever you need it.

Like this, the condition of a human is different.

But on the 6th dimensional planet, you will exist totally differently.

It is the state of having been transformed.

Depending on how many human beings can transcend their bodies when the Earth ascends its dimension, it will be decided how much the Earth can progress.

To understand "transcending the body" you can visualize the anecdote about the ascetics from the legend. Their merit, which is able to bellow that they feel too hot and steamed even when they are in the icy water, is coming from their mental strength, which had overcome from the body.

---

[1] Practice: In a general sense, it means training to acquire a certain ability or skill. However, the 'practice' referred to in Seongye Practice is the activity where a trainee repeatedly cultivates and trains one's body and mind for spiritual evolution. It is the path of true practice to accumulate pure and strong energy and purify one's surroundings with that energy through this activity.

At the abnormal level of the 6th dimension, everyone will reach the perfect state of transcending the body; and their level of dimension will be decided depending on the level of their mental part.

Even on a 6th dimensional planet, there can be 9th dimensional beings.

And also at the 9th dimensional planet, there are beings below the 9th dimension.

Inside of the fence of the same university, the freshman and senior are different, and the level of the student and professor is different. All of these are the phased learning places for evolution.

On the earth, it's like you are studying involuntarily in an imprisoned status. But after that, you will hone and polish yourself voluntarily.

Once the spirit has ascended, without any forcing, having willingness that wants to go to the perfection from imperfection and to the high dimension from the low dimension will become a natural part of daily life.

And the situation of being ruined by impulse or instinct won't happen.

When dimension is ascending higher and higher, a little difference will look bigger, and the wish of wanting to make such factors evolve will become the policy of the planet, like the policy of the nation.

Chapter 14

Cosmic Beings' Food, Clothing, Shelter and their Life and Death

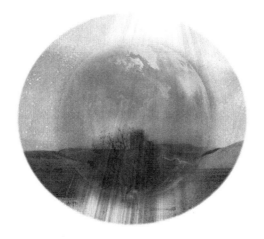

Today I am going to ask you more about the life of your planet. First of all, would you please tell me about your clothing style? I am very interested in fashion.

We wear clothes according to one's own grade. Here, clothes are the yardstick that shows one's status. Of course, they are eco-friendly. As in Taekwondo rank is indicated by yellow, blue, red and black belts, we wear different styles of clothes with different colors according to the current grade of one's soul.

Here clothes are one of the means of expressing one's status; the more evolved the race of a species is, the more graceful their clothing is. The concept might be confusing compared to that of the Earth. Rather than the overdressed and dignified costume worn by a royal family, they are more refined and graceful attires.

What is the reason why you use clothing to indicate one's grade?

That is to spark one's desire for evolution. The Universe has totally different circumstances than that of the Earth. In every factor, while the Earth can, owing to its imperfection, bear quick outcomes by drawing numerous changes from the imperfection, the Universe is made from a gigantic automated system. Once we get used to the system, we can easily maintain a comfortable condition. However, because of the comfort, some come to have no more need for further development; so for clear awareness of one's own status, it is necessary to wear clothing distinguished by one's grade.

Unlike the Earth's human beings who have physical bodies, since we cosmic beings exist in an energy state, we can't bring about dramatic change in this condition. So, by wearing corresponding attires according to grades, we can always be aware of our positions and develop the mind of admiring those who are of higher grades and can upgrade ourselves through desiring evolution

Is all right to wear the clothes one prefers to by designing them according to his/her own preference?

Of course, it doesn't matter; you can wear what you want. The Universe is the place where one's free will is respected, so there is no one who will blame you for even having a shabby look like a beggar and strolling on the street. However, the degree of evolution is manifested in every aspect, and one's status reveals one's level of practice and self-discipline outwardly, so it is customary to wear clothes which are in accordance with one's own status. In the Universe there are no cases where worn out pants are worn, where one exposes one's bust or show the shape of your body in close-fitting clothes as the youngsters of the Earth do. Those are the styles that can only exist at the place where people think highly of the value of the physical body like the Earth. In the Universe, wearing such clothing is behavior which degrades one's self on one's own and those whose meridians and acupoints are all open can't breathe and feel suffocated in those clothes.

Then, what is the criterion for beauty in your planet?

On the Earth, the criterion for beauty is biased to the beauty of appearance in many cases. On the contrary, the more highly evolved cosmic beings they are, the criterion for beauty is set by the beauty of one's mind; the barometer is how big one's love is. The inner beauty is well-refined thought and mind; especially the size of one's mind of loving all creatures in the world, makes the most representative yardstick for measuring beauty.

It is amazing to hear that the size of one's love makes the yardstick for beauty. By the way how much sleep do you have in a day? Also, would you tell me about your meals?

Since my home planet has almost perfect conditions in terms of energy compared to that of the Earth, we are always being replenished with energy. Therefore, we don't need much sleep; 1-2 hours of daily sleep is enough. As for meals too, having fresh vegetables and fruit once or twice is enough for meals.

If you rarely sleep and have simple meals, I guess your life must be considerably plain and simple.

That is right. This probably looks boring compared to that of the Earth's people, but we waste less time to that extent.

By sparing the time, what do you use the time for?

We do meditation, study some things, have conversations with others or sometime just fool around. Nevertheless, all of us are born with what we are scheduled to do from the moment of our births. Through work, we can advance our own evolution. Also since we believe we can contribute to the evolution of the group we belong to by carrying out the work, we don't waste our time in vain.

What about your housing?

The style of housing on the planet is based on about 35m², and space wider than that is unnecessary for personal use. A house for us is a space for practice and rest. As for the basic structure of a house, we can view the outer scenery from the inside, but outside people cannot look into the house.

Houses also breathe through inhalation and exhalation. Accordingly, the basic level of ventilation must be guaranteed. During the day, we can let the warm spring sunshine into the house as it comes, and so do winds. The house always keeps the temperature and humidity the same and can be controlled by an automated system. A house is another expression of one's character, so we can build our own style of houses. All of these are possible through visualization.

Is it a metropolitan residence culture such as megacities of the Earth? Or is it eco-friendly like the rural regions?

It is the culture form where nature and cutting-edge systems co-exist. Architectures applied with state-of-the-art technology are situated in nature in a beautiful harmony. Around the buildings beautiful little water falls flow and the water streams cover all the residential areas. This is the space where birds and other animals are also naturally unified with us.

Oh, that sounds like paradise; far from the current reality of the Earth. What do you think about the present forms of residence on the Earth?

A house has to have room for rest and recharge. Now the houses in the middle of big cities are for the cities themselves rather than for human beings; the modern people of the Earth are living a life of chickens in a cage.

Because human bodies constitute a part of nature, people can only recharge themselves with the necessary energy from nature. Nevertheless, contemporary men are trapped in rigid asphalt and ferro-concrete structures and it is difficult to step on breathing bare ground in their life. They are living in the optimistic environment where their bodies get stressed out, and under this situation, their immunity has no option but to become consistently feeble. As human beings became tied to materials, they got further removed from nature, and that caused the retrogression of their spirituality.

The habitation Earth's humankind has to pursue in the future is the lifestyle of co-existing with nature. Human beings can have their mental conditions purified by staying close to nature. Nature has the power to refine people's emotions. Since it faces humans with purity all the time, it helps them to keep pure minds. You have to seek a life close to nature.

I understand. I can feel many things.

Love and Marriage of Cosmic Beings

Then, how about marriage?

We respect each other's territory and strive for each one's evolution and the evolution of the entire community.

On the planet Earth, we regard such a state of marriage as a desirable relationship. What is the difference between them?

We perceive the oath with a soul as precious. Since in our society everything is operated transparently, we would never break our partner's heart or cheat on one another.

Why do the people of the Earth have love in such an immature way and tie it under a marriage system?

Due to the features of planet Earth, people approach love with the concept of possession. Since they think love or a person is an object they can own, they try to fulfill their imperfection of being alone with somebody else in the material concept of the Earth.

In the current marriage system of the Earth, people choose to get married for external factors regardless of love, such as the criteria of society or the family, material dependence or a legal solution for a sexual issue, rather than making a decision by spiritually mature people. Therefore the custom exists in a quite different form from the ideal marriage or the marriage that nurtures one's evolution.

In the current trend, increasing numbers of couples don't want to get bound to the custom of marriage, but most people think marriage is something they will do. How is it on your planet?

On my planet, marriage is optional; we don't have to get married. It is not the way of having someone else because you are alone and lonely. While we acknowledge it is one of the ways of life, many people live single.

Then, how can we describe a healthy culture of love?

Well, I can't talk about it clearly because I didn't major in love… Love I think about is about a high meeting between one being and another. In addition, that is also what we have to make effort for and cultivate for the sake of each other's evolution.

I think a powerful source of strength that moves the Universe is love and creation. Being healthy signifies the elevation of energy moving in the right direction in accordance with the flow and giving a good influence to those around you with the unimaginable energy of love. I think that love, which can transform into the love of the Universe due to the energy of mutual vitality, begins from true self-love. A liberated and independent soul who knows how to have self-love can lead their love to the development for each other in a healthy way, not with dependence.

Then, I think we could understand that a desirable culture of marriage would be the extension of such a way of love.

I agree with you. A desirable marriage culture is the process that begins from healthy culture of love and bears its fruit at last. When the Earth shifts to the 5th dimension, you will experience changes in consciousness in many areas. To tell you exactly once again, since you have changes in your consciousness, you can experience the dimensional leap to the 5th dimension.

The change in consciousness is shifting the paradigm of your life and changing your attitude for life. As the concept of love as limited to your self and opposite gender expands, the banal love confessions such as "I can't live without you!" will all disappear. Well, you would even say "I will live my life happily even without you~"

In the culture of the New Humankind in the future, the vivid steps and gestures of those who clearly know about a fruitful life and beautiful death will emerge clearly in the courageous attitude of setting one's goal and proceeding towards it. In the extension of it, the culture of marriage will be defined; however I think that how it will appear is up to all of you. I anticipate that a beautiful marriage culture will be re-written as a general marriage culture of the New Humankind.

It looks like a sagacious and happy marriage culture that suits the New Humankind will unfold beautifully after the transition period of planet Earth.

I understand. Now I want to hear about the death of cosmic beings. Many people of the Earth have much fear about death. I think the people of your planet are a bit different.

We have a lifespan of thousands to tens of thousands of years. Depending on the level of one's consciousness, cases can differ, but we mostly choose our death on our own. We choose death as a means to transfer to another circumstance for our evolution when we ascertain that there is no more progress in the wisdom we have built up for a long time.

We have previous lives and life after death; we can get connected to those lives through consciousness. In other words, when we are newly born, the memories and accumulated wisdom are revived so that we can integrate them into our consciousness. Therefore, death is not a process of sadness.

The funeral of my planet is a beautiful ceremony because we know we can converse with the soul through telepathy and the meaning of death is just traveling to other planets as a means of dimensional transfer. The funeral of our planet is the ceremony for completing the travel to the planet; all the acquaintances around the deceased get together, recollect and bless the person. We leave the soul, who must be preparing for another travel, with gratitude and songs.

On your planet, death is not sadness but another start.

Chapter 15

The Year 2025, the Future of the Earth

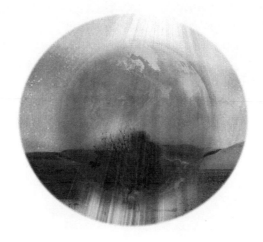

Hello, Marlin. Lastly, can we talk about the Earth in the year 2025?

First, the weather is identical throughout the year.

The color of the sky is glittering white.

The sun is not blazing anymore with the color orange,

It is a relaxed round shape like a moon.

Two suns will rise from both sides east and west and cross in the sky, and night does not exist.

The repetition of day and night is only a phenomenon that exists on the Earth.

A pretty ray belt that looks like a coat string that crosses the sky, and wraps around the earth.

A belt like Saturn's will be formed around the earth.

Asteroids surrounding the Earth will reveal themselves.

A myriad of resources and equipment will be open up to Earth's people.

It is not visible for the earthmen, but, as the earth is ascending its dimension, its locked door will open, and the Earth will be revealed to the whole universe,

Ah… the Earth is… so beautiful even now,

But it is even more beautiful than it seems…

Somehow, the pretty shape of marble is flashing into my mind.

Yes, I guess the features of the Earth would look exactly like that.

The solar system will ascend several steps from this point.

Because space and time will be open, it will be possible to interchange with other planets at any time.

And, right now, there are lots of cosmic beings who were born on the Earth, thus there will be active interchange between their home planets.

The ocean will change to be like a pure lake, and its function will be air purification and Water Element supply.

There would be no huge water space like the Pacific as it is now.

The land will be enlarged thus enormously large ground will be formed,

The population is far smaller than now, and the civilization will be living together somewhere,

And the rest of the areas will just exist as nature.

The animals and plants will become much simpler than now.

Beings from the Universe who had completed their roles on the Earth, will have gone back to their home planets, so on the Earth, the animals and plants will be rearranged with the species that perform appropriate roles for Earth people's level.

While going through the Grand Earth Project, almost every species will be in the process of arrangement for some time, and according to the planning chart of the Book of Life, the Earth will have its creatures rearranged.

Closing my eyes and visualizing that, it is so beautiful.

Even if all of these are just my imagination, I will take it as a gift for my conversation with you.

Yes, it is the world where everything is accomplished when you visualize.

It is not something imaginary at all. Conversely, if it does not happen as expected, that is considered to be strange, and even that is the situation which indicates big trouble.

What kind of the house will we live in?

The housing will be changed so much from now.

The population will not be as big as it is now, and such structures as apartments no longer exist.

Skyscrapers, as I have told you before, are only built when they have symbolic meanings.

In many cases the residences are located inside the planet.

It is the optimum space that is best for sleeping and having a rest.

The solar energy is supplied even to the inner space, thus the shortage of energy, or receiving insufficient light will never happen.

I'm sure that the human's lifestyle would change, wouldn't it?

What kind of clothes will we wear?

It's just a piece of thin cloth.

It is very similar to the outfits of Rome and old Korean dynasty, but it is not something that is drooping all over. It is not an overexposed wear, but it is simple wear. Neck and arms are naturally bared, and it is made from the fiber that is as light as possible.

Do we make our own clothes? Or is there a store for selling them?

The economic life of human beings will change so much. There isn't any department store or shop.

A person will be connected to a specialist who makes clothes that fit that person well, thus it will be changed into a tailor-made system. To have clothes made would not be as inconvenient as it is now.

It will use the minimum buttons and decorations, so it's very convenient to take it on and off.

But it is made from a functional fiber, thus it naturally keeps itself clean.

It does not even need to be washed.

It is breathable and absorbs sweat effectively.

Once it has fulfilled its lifetime, a recycling machine will dispose of it, and it will quickly go back to the form of the original element so that it will be utilized for a new creation. This is the structure of how it will work.

Ah... After going through the Earth's great change, I will be able to live as a beautiful and evolved citizen of the Universe. This must be the figure of paradise that human beings have dreamed about from the beginning.

It is truly a beautiful Universe.

Unfortunately, now it is time to conclude our conversation.

While I'm conversing with you, I'm not really sure how far I have approached the infinity of the Universe that is drawn endlessly, even though I pull it ceaselessly!

It is the same here too.

We are more opened to the information than Earth people, so we are in the position of delivering information; nevertheless whenever we get to know more, and whenever we talk more about it, we feel like we don't know enough about the Universe.

We know things within the range of our knowledge, so we are diffident especially when we think that it would be at least 1% of the Universe. However, we are trying to know and are stepping towards it gradually, at least one step at a time. I consider being born to be a fruitful thing

Yes, you are absolutely right.

I sincerely thank you for showing me the magnificence of the Universe and also being together with me. While we were talking together, I was vibrating with joy and I felt happy.

We thank you too.

Lastly, can I ask if you have a message for Earth's people?

Sure. We love the Earth and I would like to say that all creations on the Earth are so precious. The valuable time we have spent communicating with our Earth friends is our love of the Earth and towards Earth's people. I hope you will remember our love. If you are sharing our love with all creations that exist on the Earth, to love and care for them, we would be most grateful. We will be always with you. Call us anytime when you need help. We will always cheer and support you. We love you, Earth friends!

Chapter 16

Adapting to the Earth's Great Change While Overcoming the Crisis

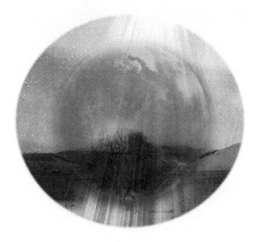

If with concern you put things into action one by one and arouse your interest and love for the Earth and living things, that will be a solution. Love may sound unreal, but it is a very real method.

Individual, Corporate and National Guidelines for Overcoming Crises

What must be prepared at the national level in order to get over this crisis and adapt ourselves to the great change of the Earth?

First of all, countries must recognize and accept these critical situations correctly. Each country must take action for the safety and survival of its people. The paradigm that has operated the nation and led society until now has no option but to replace itself. The only way to calm down the Earth, which has already begun its powerful self-cleansing process is for mankind to alter their consciousness and awaken to live together with animals, plants and all beings on the Earth as soon as possible.

Also each country should let their people know about the future and urge them to prepare themselves. People must be taught about what the Earth and human beings will look like after their dimensions have been promoted and about what they will need, in order to live through that stage. Also not to be dragged down by falling economic indicators, nations must make every effort to change their people's consciousness.

What policies should countries adopt right now?

Present situations cannot be dealt with in the usual ways of national administration. The industries that overuse resources or energy must be replaced or converted immediately. In particular, the types of business that discharge a large amount of substances causing global warming must be regulated right away. People must be enlightened to lead lives that are sound and do not harm nature. And the industrial systems must be made to steer their directions in revolutionary ways in order to harmonize with the ways of people's lives.

In addition, in order for the people to be born again as the new mankind, more active efforts must be made in the cultural industries than any other areas. To help people awaken spiritually, the consumptive and seductive culture of capitalism need to be totally revised, and this needs to be supported with national policies.

Nations need to store food, drinking water, medicine, etc to provide for their people. Since transportation networks will highly likely not work due to nationwide disasters, food-storing facilities must be built in major areas and in granaries.

As for medicine, mainly western medicines should be prepared as usual. But it is necessary to study herbs as an alternative medicine and you should grow and provide them. Additionally, people must be taught self-curing methods such as acupuncture and moxibustion. They should be able to obtain herbs easily around them so that they can survive in isolation in critical situations for at least a few years.

Drinking water is an especially important matter. Probably the present urban water supply facilities will not work well. If the pipelines are broken by even a weak earthquake, the whole urban water supply can be disturbed. When disasters come, drinking water will be polluted and contagious diseases will more than likely be spread through water. It is also necessary to develop efficient ways to utilize underground water and to purify the water of streams and rivers.

Above all, present concentrated urban systems and housing must be avoided, and people need to be guided to make a foundation for their livelihood and find a means of living outside the cities for themselves.

These are probably the policies that will be difficult for any government to carry out. However, governments must keep it in mind that tremendous earthquakes and tidal waves, and droughts and floods will keep coming and that stored food and drinking water will run out soon within one or two years. If they are still attached to immediate economic or political interests, they will not able to solve such problems by any means. It is more important than anything else for governors to have a thorough awareness about such situations.

What can companies do? Are there any measures they can take?

Companies must change their ways of thinking. Up until now companies have made every effort to only make profits. Therefore, it is the companies that have made the Earth suffer a lot. From now on companies should take action to save people. The policies mentioned before cannot be carried out only by governments. Governments, companies and people also have to work together and execute them. The managers of companies need to be able to move their companies not to make their own profits but to save people. Only when the companies give up their own profit so as to survive together, will they be able to expect their new future.

What kind of preparation and guidelines for their action do individuals need?

If governments play their roles properly, many things will be able to be prepared if individuals work along with their government. But considering the rigidity of governments, it is far more important for individuals to change their consciousness and become prepared.

People must begin by changing their consciousness. They should not live only for themselves, for their family or furthermore for other human beings, but they should also reflect on their position as hosts who live together with all animals, plants and the Earth and should realize now what they must do. They need clarity and self-awareness about important issues in their lives.

In other words, people must think over their life purposes and change their way of living. One's life is given in order for one to grow and evolve through experience, and material things are only a means for the evolution. People should not be attached to materials, and they must reduce the burdens they have laid on the Earth by changing their consumption-oriented lifestyles and by minimizing garbage. Also, they need to actively share their own understanding with others.

Furthermore, they have to know why these sufferings are given to mankind now. They must understand that these sufferings are not just to make human beings feel pain but to facilitate their rebirth into more mature spiritual entities.

Eco-communities: Living for Co-existence and Awakening!

It was mentioned before that human beings have to change their ways of living in order to overcome the crisis. In what way should they convert their lives?

The present economic system of the Earth has the goal of pursuing profits through mass manufacturing and consumption. In this system, materials are of great value and it is difficult for human beings, nature and the environment to remain in their original state. We can say that eco-communities are the correct way of living, and are the way to solve the problems the Earth faces now.

In fact, living does not require as many materials as people think. Plain food, simple and neat clothes and a small house are enough. What humans really need is mental sharing, spiritual affluence and evolution through the fundamental questions of why we are alive. People work together, produce as many goods and food as they need, and share what they have. In this way people can exist together with nature.

Living in such eco-communities, people will have to change their life styles completely. They are likely to feel afraid of such changes.

Humans have a fundamental thirst for freedom in their mind and they may be unwilling to be controlled or to abide by given rules. This shows that humans have their own free will. If they understand that living in eco-communities consists of the culture that respects humans' free will, these problems will be solved. It is necessary to understand that living in eco-communities is a more advanced way of living.

People of higher levels spontaneously develop the need for understanding about others and sharing with them, while those of lower levels are likely to hide within themselves and have difficulty communicating with others. Living in a community is a way of living in which people expand their energy through exchange and harmony among people and make efforts to advance together. Also this way of living can solve the problems of the limited materialistic life the current mankind faces and the problems of limited resources and environment which the Earth possesses.

If people plant and grow life together, in nature in this way, it will help them to become awakened.

That's right. Soil is a means as well as a material that the Creator made in order to make and grow living things. All the energies to conceive and grow life are condensed into the soil of the material world. Animals are made through soil, plants grow on soil, even human beings are given life and grow up based on soil. We can say soil is a treasure warehouse of life as well as a storage place for food can't we?

When humans meet and touch soil, they are designed to awaken to their original consciousness of life that they have had since they originally took root on the Earth. When they moved away from the soil, human tragedy began. At the moment when people touch soil, they resonate with the original consciousness of life that is enshrined in their DNAs, even though it has now degenerated. There is no better means than soil to awaken the consciousness of human beings who come out of soil and return to it.

Break Through Crises using Mankind's Collective Unconscious

To break through the present situations effectively, besides the effort to change the way of living it looks like the awakening of each one matters, and in addition the condition of the consciousness of the whole of mankind is more important than anything else. What do you think of the present state of mankind?

The waves and phenomena of the Earth are of great concern even in the Universe, so we have also inspected and analyzed mankind's collective unconscious and events on the Earth in great detail. It is not only culture that forms the collective consciousness of human beings. For example, children will burst into tears when they are taken high up somewhere, not because they had fallen down before but because their genes contain the memory inherited from their ancestors. This can be called the collective unconscious. Like this, human unconsciousness has been formed for so long, so it is close to instinct. This instinctive unconsciousness is so strong that it can make humans forget about all the information passed on through education or culture.

Do you see the collective unconscious of people on the Earth?

Yes, I do. Though it is complex, I see it clearly. The collective unconscious of the present mankind is in a serious condition and it is the same as being driven into a deadlock. Even though the internet and the development of various contents make some things appear to happen actively, weariness gradually takes root in the mind of human beings, so they have strong unwillingness to do anything. Many cases of depression and suicide take place out of weariness in the collective unconscious.

People lose interest in whatever they do because they are caught in the feeling that their tedious living will continue and days will be endlessly repeated if something new doesn't pop up. This is weariness. In the future, humans' collective unconscious of this weariness and torpor will increase. Such consciousness will lead people to get so frustrated and depressed as to choose suicide or to do cruel things in order to stay alive, out of survival instincts when the crisis arrives. Those are of no help to anyone.

Then how can we change the collective unconscious which is in this state?

You can appeal to the unconscious. Talk directly to the unconscious beyond human logic. Don't try to set up theories on it, but let it be spontaneously established as a culture. Human beings have already known that and their minds are longing for change. It is only human living which is surrounded by social systems and economic logic which keeps such minds from being displayed outwardly.

In which direction must the humans' collective unconscious be changed?

You can see the collective unconscious is none other than the mind of the entire mankind; the best direction is towards love. You may regard it as too commonplace, however humans think like that because they don't know the mechanism of love clearly. Love is the best solution.

The Energy of Love That Saves the Earth

You said that we should change mankind's collective unconscious with love. Would you please tell me more about the energy of love specifically?

Although love can be expressed in many different ways, its energy is all the same. That is – vital life force. Loving people brim with life and a loving society is full of vitality. Love is the energy that runs the Universe. It is the fundamental power that makes the very core of all things. If we say the first stage of love is the love between man and woman, new lives are born out of that love. Love is the energy that creates such lives.

Secondarily, if love is directed toward people, not only between a man and a woman, the love brings about the development of consciousness. That is people don't live by human instinct only but develop their inclination to the path of evolution. As people come to know what they should do on the stage named "Earth", they will be reborn as conscious entities from being just natural beings.

Next, when love is exalted to the dimension of love for nature, people become aware not just of visible lives but of invisible ones. If you feel like saying hello to animals and plants, you have already begun to believe in invisible beings. If you feel the love of plants that is full of pure love, you will become conscious of the circulation system of the Earth and will be in communion with family members of the living entity, the Earth.

Next comes the love for Heaven. Then you will enter the stage where you realize why you were born on the Earth and what you have to do on the Earth. Then you will finally develop consciousness about the Universe and begin to seriously think about the question "Who am I?". Your love is then promoted to the level of the Universe.

Like this, love may be in many different levels, but we can say it is all the same in the point that the energy called love creates new life forces.

If the consciousness of humanity grows and their love increases, can we change the situation of the pending crisis?

The land cannot be restored even if you realize its value after you have ruined it. Likewise, you will have to go through what you have to but the intensity of the crisis can be decreased. If many people recognize and love the Earth as a living entity, they will be able to recognize the signals of the Earth. When they can converse with the Earth, they will be able to discuss the situations with the Earth. They will be able to evacuate in advance because they will be able to receive information about the impending volcanic eruptions. They will be able to know about coming disasters so deaths will decrease.

For instance, listen to the Earth now. The Earth says that since the balance and harmony of its circulation systems are broken, it laments its serious illness and says that it can hardly control the system anymore. She says as a result of that, the atmosphere is full of Fire energy, so global warming and abnormal weather conditions are brought about.

What can we do for Mother Earth who groans with serious illness?

At first, we should feel sincerely sorry towards Mother Earth who has almost died because of her children who lack good sense, and we should apologize to her. And then, we should think about how to cure her. If Fire energy is the problem, you can pull it down and make use of it; that is, you can farm or grow plants. In a place where anything grows, Fire energy is necessary for them to grow, so Fire energy flows down to that place naturally. So if the Fire energy of the Earth diminishes, plants will grow. Because of the destruction of the Amazon, Fire energy has lost its method to be released. That has triggered the boost of the Earth's self-purification function. Growing life through safeguarding farming and planting forests can be one of the healing methods for the Earth.

If you act with concern one by one in this way and stir up your interest and love for the Earth and living things, this will be a solution. Love may sound unreal, but it is a very real method. In order to overcome the present crisis, humankind must fall in love with the Earth. It is love.

If you understand and love the earth sincerely, and don't think only about survival because of fear, the energy of the love will make you act unconsciously and that will make everything grow. If the actions and minds of such love are continued in succession like dominoes and become the entire consciousness of mankind, the Earth would cease its violent self-cleansing. Furthermore, the power of such love will be the source from which mankind will be born as the heroes of the new age.

We cosmic beings are waiting for the humankind of the Earth to wake up. We would like to help you overcome the pending crisis well and make a leap to the new age. We would like to deliver our good intentions through this conversation, because you human beings and we cosmic beings are companions and brothers and sisters of the Universe… We really hope that it will not be too late for you to wake up.

We appreciate your concern and good intentions for the Earth and human beings. From now on, let us begin our sincere love for Mother Earth.

Epilogue

Well, we've come to the end of the book.

How do you feel?

After having these conversations, I came to know that people who live on the Earth in this very period were standing in front of a time of special destiny. The Earth has already entered the time of the great change and one thing that is obvious is that everyone will be subjected to the change, no matter whether they want it or not.

The messages of the cosmic beings don't intend to deliver threatening situations or random optimistic hope to us, but rather, they are trying to awaken the change in us, the Earth's people.

For me, while having these conversations, tiny changes began to grow in reality, in my mind and daily life. Even when I used a cup of water or a sheet of paper, I came to consider the environmental influence my action creates somewhere on the Earth. The Earth is no longer just ground that I step on absent-mindedly, and the pain of the Earth as a mother which is alive, was passed on to me. Each continent is no longer a remote place thousands of miles away where strangers live, but now I have developed affection and concern for their lives and cultures. We are one family who have been cultivating the history and civilization of the Earth together.

The Cosmic Beings don't wish you to feel heavy, nor do they wish you to feel elated. It's necessary to have the facts before you move forward.

It is now the time to face what is coming–straight on. We are mature humans, and can therefore take responsibility for what we have created. These messages came from love. Like a baby that cries as it comes out of love, the Universe is giving you the opportunity to be reborn. Will you take part in this rebirth? The choice is fully yours.

As free will is yours, you can choose to ignore this and live your life freely without the burden of doing something about this information. Or, you can choose to participate in the evolution of the Earth and the salvation of its families. In the latter case, it's necessary that you begin to listen to nature and feel its pains that are being expressed all around us. If you could hear the cries of the ground, sea, soil, plants and animals that are without the clean environment they need in order to live, wouldn't you cry too?

Then make a conscious decision to be aware of the Earth during your day, and share your feelings and actions with others. Your love for nature and your love to share is probably the fastest solution to the crisis of the Earth.

But that is only a start.

The crisis will escalate over the year and get worse next year. That means that we can no longer live the way we did before. We can no longer let our collective unconscious rule our lives.

Like breaking an addiction, we must let go of the weariness of our tired bodies and minds. Wake up!

Now! Yes! You!

There can be no more excuses. If you believe now is the time, then stand up and express your love. We must move toward eco-friendly living and eco-communities. Before, it used to be an alternative lifestyle choice, now it's a question of universal survival.

Cut down on unnecessary consumption and on creating excessive garbage, and rather, save our resources.

This book is a call for us to wake up and join forces together to share this information and create a movement to change the collective unconscious of the Earth.

Let's give Mother Earth some hope by showing her that we can change our living patterns. Together we can overcome the crisis of this material civilization and enter into a new kind of living and in doing so, save ourselves and the Earth.

It looks like we need accurate recognition about what's happening on the Earth now. If we understand the situation only superficially, we will be highly likely to apply just quick fixes and that will result in constant frustration. We have to view the current situation and seek for our way forward in the dimension of the entire Earth and from the viewpoint of the mankind, don't we?

After that, the actual change has to begin from our minds and then be followed by our actions. For a change of our life, it seems like we have to strive to bring about the change of our society and all mankind, starting from taking small actions.

To sum up, before we ask somebody else what to do, the best shortcut to change all of us is that we first check what each of us is putting into action now.

The planet Earth which has spent eons of time just as a planet at the corner of a solar system is now about to ascend to the 5th dimension, to the main stage of the Universe, transcending its stage of just being a little planet at the corner of the solar system. This is a blessing given to Earth's humanity.

However, the severe growing pains we will go through in the process requires the awakening and clear awareness of all of us. Do we really have the power to overcome the hardship? If yes, where would this power come from...?

I believe it is Love...

Wouldn't it be love that rises up from the depths of human beings? I think with the love, full of vitality, the world can change even today and our mankind can head for light in the middle of this darkness.

Now we don't have much time. For what do we hesitate and what more do we need to wait for?

It is the coming of the world that we have always dreamt of.

Let's put small actions into practice and deliver this message to our neighbours and the family of the Earth in order to create a great surge of change.

33 Ways of Practicing Love to Save the Earth and it's Family.

1. I will live in a "hot" way during the summer at 26 degrees Celsius and in a "cool" way during the winter at 22 degrees–boilers and air conditioners are hippos that gulp energy.

2. I will thoroughly abide by garbage recycling–if each individual recycles even just one thing, then 7 billion pieces of garbage will be recycled.

3. I will unplug electronic devices–the consumption of standby electricity is bigger than that of the energy I use for the device itself.

4. I won't leave leftovers–even now people are dying in Africa from famine.

5. I will put off unnecessary light bulbs immediately–I won't leave the light bulbs on to be less lonely.

6. I will use a handkerchief instead of tissues–a handkerchief in one's pocket is the etiquette of modern people.

7. I will recycle used paper by preparing a reusable paper box to save trees.

8. I won't use paper cups–trees are oxygen generators.

9. I will walk if my destination is not far–I can serve two ends: health and the saving of energy.

10. I won't suddenly accelerate or brake when I drive–sudden acceleration uses gas like water.

11. I will eat local foods rather than imported ones–importation of foods create enormous amount of carbon.

12. I won't eat fast food that provides the cause of environmental destruction–it is also not good for one's health.

13. I will recommend vegetables to my acquaintances who love meat, saying they are also delicious–because animals are living beings with the same right to their lives as human beings have.

14. I will use reusable bags for groceries–plastic bags don't decay for over 100 years.

15. I won't use wrappers for gifts–unnecessary wrappers pollute the environment.

16. I won't wear fur–animals lives are equivalent to human beings.

17. I won't pick flowers in a field carelessly–I will protect plants.

18. I will turn off the faucet tap when I brush my teeth or wash my hands –I will cut down the use of water.

19. I will purchase refill goods if I have the case–plastics don't decay.

20. I will quit smoking–it contaminates air and is harmful to the health of people around me.

21. I won't use paper towels–I will save trees.

22. I will collect the garbage around my house–this is the beginning of environmental protection.

23. I won't use kitchen items which are harmful to the environment, such as bleached coffee filters or plastic wraps–they don't decay.

24. I won't buy unnecessary stuff–I won't buy things because they are on sale.

25. I will save, share, swop and re-use goods–recycling is the beginning of environmental protection.

26. I will use cotton diapers and sanitary pads rather than disposable ones–disposable goods bruise the Earth.

27. I will grow vegetables in my garden or balcony–it is also good for one's mental health.

28. I will use organic goods–if we reduce the usage of chemicals, the soil will recover.

29. I will use stairs instead of elevators–I can take care of my health as well as save energy.

30. I will set my own "green mentor" and I will try to imitate their actions and share my actions with others–acts with honorable people are enjoyable.

31. I will use or donate my time and money for the environment–it is exciting to help others perform good deeds.

32. I will pray for the Earth every day–I will participate in changing the collective unconscious.

33. I will wear long johns in the winter seasons–that allows me to save 10% of heating energy.

Appendix

Introducing the Planets involved in the Conversations

The Earth

It is the planet of 3rd dimension. It is located between Sagittarius and Coma Berenices of our galaxy. It is the 4th planet (including the sun) of the solar system. Its grade is 7.8. The Earth is a school planet famous for its high level of difficulty; due to its diversity and co-existence of good and evil, it makes human emotion go to the extreme. Also, it has the rule of reincarnation. Since there are various kinds of waves and energy on this planet, its level of vital energy is higher than its grade; the level amounts to that of grade 8.9 planet. So, it is a planet of quick progress in training.

Pleiades

It is the planet of the 6th dimension. It is located in Taurus. Its grade is 8.6. Taurus is composed of 7 stars. Pleiades has evolved from material civilization to spiritual civilization so as to provide direct help to the Earth when the Earth has a dimension leap. The beings of Pleiades are well-versed in the emotion of the people of the Earth.

About Suseonjae

"Why does my life go this way?"

This might occur to anyone when we feel gloomy or when something hard happens to us. Meanwhile, when things turn out fine, we put aside such an idea in a corner of our minds and we forget about it and just go back to our life again. Then if we bump into the difficulties again, we repeat dwelling on our own misfortune. This is the appearance of common people's life. Consequently, at the end of our life, we slap our laps and realize there was something we didn't know throughout our whole life, something we should have definitely known before we pass away.

"What is the true meaning of my life?"

"What is the true life of a human being?"

Suseonjae is the meditation school where modern people who live with such fundamental but unsolved questions in their heart can find the true meaning of their life.

A younger brother who was responsible for his bothers accidental death, found inner healing, a young female teacher who is taking charge of a class with troublemakers in a boys school but says she is learning more from the kids, a painter who is living a life in nature while cultivating an animal farm after overcoming an ovarian cancer, a career woman who came to learn the true taste of life as she started to live in a countryside after 10 years of professional work in a big city and an American guy who acquired the skill of how to cook as tasty a soy bean paste soup as Koreans do… This is the place with special people who are living common lives.

They have restored their relationships with their disconnected inner self, neighbours, nature and the Universe, through meditation and are recovering the true happiness in the centre of oneness within themselves. Also, they are living the life practicing how human beings co-exist with creations of nature, while passing on the truth they realized through meditation, to neighbours and the world.

Operation of Life Museums: Seon Culture Experience Center

What is life and what is death?

How do I live my life?

These are the questions numerous people are desperately searching for answers to nowadays.

Increasing numbers of middle-aged people and elders as well as young ones are wandering about losing their life paths.

Essentially, humans, nature, Heaven and the Universe came out of "one," and they have cultivated the Earth into a beautiful and abundant planet of life while helping one another. However, as the material civilization empowers its influence, humans have gradually been further removed from other beings and have built an egoistic civilization only for their own good. As the result, our Earth is suffering from an incurable disease and all creatures of nature and the Universe are sending warnings to human beings. Suseonjae's Seon Culture Experience Center is a life museum to inform people of the mistakes that have brought such a crisis to the Earth and suggest the model of life where we can love and vitalize each other.

Seon Culture Promotion & Education Center

Teaching People about a Fruitful Life and a Beautiful Death

SPEC is the area for life education to teach people how to live a fruitful life and how to prepare for a beautiful death. It is a nonprofit organization established by people including meditation experts, art mind healers, and organic farming specialists. "Seon" is the condition where people-nature-the Universe co-exist in harmony. Even though good spiritual teachings are overflowing in the world, they are not of much help for the public because they only approach the essence partly.

To accomplish a fruitful life and a beautiful death, we need both knowledge and love for people, nature and Heaven. The true path of life can be found when we practice love for human beings, love for nature and love for Heaven. SPEC is the integrated education arena to promote teachings for life through the Seon Culture.

Also, to spread the recovery of nature and a desirable funeral culture based on right understanding about life and death, SPEC is engaging in various movements through "Getting rid of tombs, "Organ donation and hospice, and the "The cultivation of eco-friendly grave yards"

Suseonjae webpage

www.suseonjae.org

About Roar Sheppard

Roar Sheppard was born in 1972. He is American and has been residing in Korea for about 15 years. While staying in Korea, he has studied Korean traditional culture and language. He was interested in the secret of the Universe and searched for it through meditation. Meditation and the breathing training have been his daily routine for 8 years and through the deep silence of his training he began to hear the pains of plants, expressed through their wavelengths. Over time he felt he could communicate with various beings in nature then suddenly came to converse with Marlin, a cosmic being of Pleiades.

Marlin

He is a cosmic being from Pleiades. His specialty is forecasting the future and he is especially interested in the planet Earth. This comic being who has blonde hair and blue eyes and is 186cm high is full of love and humor. He smiles a lot even at trivial things. Also, he thinks highly of attitude and manners. He is trying to send the message that if we don't change now, the Earth can become dangerous. He is praying for our evolution and that of the Earth.

If you enjoyed this book (and naturally we hope that you did) we recommend the following titles for your further reading enjoyment.

Most of Kima Global's titles are also published as eReader editions and are available on Amazon's Kindle, the Barnes & Noble Nook and other readers.

Rising out of Chaos–The New Heaven and the New Earth

by **Simon Peter Fuller**

This wonderful and inspiring book carries much the same energy as *Breath of Light*. It includes much on the early religious movements including the Essenes and the Cathars and the influence they have on modern thought.

It also includes the complete text and interpretations of Revelation III, the third book of the Apocalypse excised by the Council of Nicea in about 350CE. What it reveals gives a completely new slant on what John the Divine intended revealing the exact nature of Second Coming so relevant to today's world and the challenges we face.

ISBN 0-9584065-4-5

The Role of Evil in Human Evolution–Exposing the Dark to Light

by **David Ash**

A fresh look by British physicist and spiritual teacher David Ash at the huge influence that Churchianity has had on the world for more than 3000 years.

The author has a close look at the actions and intent of the demigod Jehovah's commanding and certainly not benevolent influence over the centuries. He has had access to early religious documents such as the Talmud and other sources.

This is a revealing and empowering read.

ISBN 978-0-9802561-3-0

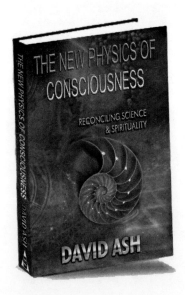

The New Physics of Consciousness– Reconciling Science and Spirituality.

by **David Ash**

David introduces a new paradigm which integrates science and spirituality. An easy rewrite of physics leads to a profound philosophy. Clear analogies and simple diagrams make the science understandable and enthralling. A Theory for everything emerges which both simple and brilliant.

Supernova explosions in distant galaxies provide proof for the theory. A new vision of matter sits with a fresh understanding of God-science and religion reconciled!

ISBN 978-0-9802561-2-3

Kima Global Publishers,
is an independent
publishing company based
in Cape Town, specialise in
Books that Make a Differ-
ence to People's Lives.

We have a unique variety of
Body, Mind and Spirit titles
that are distributed through-
out South Africa, the U.K.,
Europe, Australia and the
U.S.A.

Among our titles you will
find non-fiction topics on:
Alternative Healing,
Wellness, Philosophy,
Parenting, Business coaching,
Personal Development, Civil
Society, Environmental,
Creative workbooks and
Visionary / fantasy fiction.

http://www.kimaglobal.co.za
http://kimaglobal.spruz.com
email to: info@kimaglobal.co.za

CPSIA information can be obtained at www.ICGtesting.com
Printed in the USA
BVOW021454071011

273068BV00001B/4/P